Secrets of Attorney Marketing
Law School <u>Dares Not Teach</u>

(3rd Edition – 2022 Update)

by Richard Jacobs

ISBN: 978-1-951149-51-2

Design and Published by:

Jacobs & Whitehall
21750 Hardy Oak Blvd
Suite 104
#51700
San Antonio, Texas 78258
www.jacobsandwhitehall.com
(888) 570-7338

Warning & Disclaimer

The intent of this book is to be informational in nature only.

Marketing techniques described herein may be found to be unethical by your local or State Bar Association, or they may be prohibited under local, state, or federal laws – it's your job to check this.

Laws change, times change, and you must do your due diligence to ensure that following any of the marketing techniques in this book will not cause you legal or tax problems, or put you in conflict with your local or state Bar association. No legal or tax advice is being given by the author, publisher, or anyone associated with this work.

Publisher, author, and all parties associated with this work are unaware of any material conflicts or issues that the implementation of these marketing techniques described herein may have or cause. This book is purely informational in nature, not to be taken as an instruction manual.

The effectiveness of the techniques described in this book cannot be guaranteed, especially if implemented improperly or half-heartedly. The techniques may boost your sales, have no effect, or even hurt your sales. The author and all parties involved in this publication take no responsibility for any outcome if you choose to use this material.

For legal advice, consult a qualified attorney. For tax advice, consult a qualified tax professional.

Testimonials

"Great Ideas On Marketing! You Hit The Nail On The Head."

"I have just finished reading your book and I have to say I am impressed with your marketing ideas. I have been in private practice, criminal and domestic, for about 3 years and have gone through many different marketing plans, schemes, and downright thefts that have occurred by some organizations that promise the moon and deliver nothing.

I have tried lead generators, SEO, billboards, pay per click and direct mail marketing. Most have failed miserably. I agree with your assessment that slower but effective plans work better. Big trees need big roots. I have already changed my firm's approach and have begun to see the payoff.

You hit the nail on the head with your tracking advice. In looking back on three years of trial and error I realized I could have dumped bad ideas faster once I realized they were not working. Lesson learned, and now we are tracking the source of our leads.

I found your advice on answering the phone and scripting particularly helpful. The ability to hear my staff's interactions with clients is crucial to seeing which staff member is better at handling new prospects. I have made my staff read that section to improve customer service. It is not just the lawyer who needs to change but the whole staff needs to be on the same page.

I keep your book by my desk and constantly refer to it as a source for new ideas. Turning a talk into a book is next on the agenda and hope to have a new one linked to the website soon. Thanks for the ideas!"   **- David E. Boyle**

****

"Great, Logical Marketing Tips That You Wouldn't Think Of"

"This was an excellent book on Marketing. And a very quick read - took me a day. Not quite "secrets", but many tips in here that seem like common sense after you read it. Richard has done an amazing job spelling things out in the book. After reading it, I actually made an appointment to speak with Richard about how he could help my site. I loved his no-nonsense attitude in the book and during our meeting. He is a straight-shooter and doesn't really fluff.

One of the other reviews mentioned that the book was a lot of fluff and the book could be boiled down to 10-15 pages, but I disagree. I think the "fluff" is extra information that I believe is helpful to allowing the reader to perform these tasks on their own. Highly recommended. I've even given a few colleagues my copy to read."   **- Matthew Murillo**

****

"Get The Book, Read It, Call Richard, and Have A Conversation"

"This 175-page book provided me with some new or better ways of marketing my law practice than what I've been doing for the past 20 years. I read, tabbed and made notes prior to visiting with Richard Jacobs by phone this afternoon, so as not to waste any of his time. You should know that not once did the subject of money come up in our conversation. Still, we'll have to get around to that eventually because I'm sure he's not a non-profit company.

The book is an easy read and really shares relevant information on different ways to reach the consumer. It discusses SEO, mailers, etc. and perhaps even more importantly, how you track whether it's making you money. I'm looking forward to our next conversation!"

- Denis H. White, Jr.

****

"Excellent And Practical Marketing Concepts - I Recommend This Book"

"As an attorney in practice for over 25 years, I have studied and incorporated a number of marketing tools and approached for my practice. I have also worked with a few marketing companies. As such, I was interested to check out and read through the book. The concepts and points made in the book are excellent.

The author, Richard Jacobs, takes a practical approach to the marketing of a law firm. Many of the concepts presented can be incorporated immediately and some will take some time to implement but are certainly achievable. I recommend this book."

- David Wolf, Child Injury Lawyer

****

"Unless You Have More Law Business Than You Can Handle, You Need This Book!"

"I consider Mr. Jacobs' book to be one of the more practical and useful books on Marketing for Attorneys that is out there. It is chock full of easy to understand and implement practical ideas and roadmaps for increasing an attorney's business, especially for sole practitioners and small law offices business.

Unless you do not care about increasing your income from practicing law, this book is for you! The best part of reading Mr. Jacob's book is that it is written in a way that is enjoyable and fun to read and put to immediate use. It is the opposite of "dull!" Get this book!"

- Robert H. Tourtelot

****

"Outstanding. Enjoyed It."

"I don't think I ever gave a review for a book. The book is short and well written. This guy is outstanding. I really enjoyed reading because I enjoy the business aspect of marketing law firms.

When I first started practicing law, the yellow pages ran things. Now that Google balanced the playing field, this guy explains how to compete with Google. I get at least one SEO guy a week trying to sell me something; this is the first guy I can say that actually knows what he is talking about. I still have not hired him to handle my stuff but when I am ready (still learning) this is the guy I will go to."

- Mark Rollins

****

"Interesting and Practical Guide To Growing Your Law Business"

"Whether you're just starting your law practice or have been practicing for years, this book is a terrific resource for practical marketing ideas. Mr. Jacobs lays out how customer service and smart SEO can grow your law practice. He also outlines how easy it can be to add a large volume of quality, relevant content to your website, thereby boosting your organic SEO.

This book will force you to examine and reconsider your marketing if you are serious about increasing your business and growing your practice."

- Amy Chapman, Esq.

****

"Great Strategies For Legal Marketing"

"Richard's knowledge of attorney marketing goes far beyond any of the other legal marketers we have ever worked with. His book reveals marketing secrets that have provided tremendous benefit to our firm. He has his finger on the pulse of the legal markets and this book was a tremendous help for our marketing needs."

- Marc Grossman, Esq.

****

"Real Advice For Real Attorneys That Gets Real Results"

"Real advice for real attorneys that gets real results. Richard's book is starkly different than most of the marketing advice out there for attorneys. It is targeted at smaller firms and solos and really attacks the problems faced by these entities.

Definitely worth a read and the ideas will stay with you and become a significant part of your marketing mix. An extra bonus is the author's accessibility and willingness to answer any follow up questions you have. It's nice to see a professional so focused on the success of his clients."

- Josh Reinitz, Esq.

****

"A Good And Quick Read With Several Actionable Ideas To Grow Business"

"I thought this was a great book. It really gave me several things to think about in terms of growing my practice. He sets forth concrete and actionable ideas. They are straightforward, legal and if you think about it truly make sense.

It's a wonder so many of us have missed them through the years (or just refuse to make the effort). You're given the choice whether to implement them yourself or use the author's firm. I'm still deciding how to proceed but regardless there are great ideas in here that when put into practice can't help but increase business."

- Gabriel Katzner, Esq.

****

ABOUT THE AUTHOR

Richard Jacobs is the author of four books:

- **"But I Only Had 2 Beers!"**
  (Truth Talk from Over 25 DUI Lawyers)
- **Secrets of Attorney Marketing Law School Dares Not Teach**
  (1st, 2nd, and 3rd Editions)
- **The Ultimate Guide to Local Business Marketing (Published**
  by Entrepreneur Press; Richard Jacobs (co-author))

Richard has spoken about Law Firm marketing at:

- NACDL Las Vegas DUI Conference (Private session held
  during the conference)
- PILMMA (Personal Injury Lawyers Marketing &
  Management Association)
- DUIDLA Arizona Conference
- Perry Marshall & Associates Small Business Marketing
  Conference

Richard specializes in helping attorneys break free from 70
hour work weeks and marginal law practices. Through his
work at Speakeasy Marketing, Inc, he helps hundreds of
attorneys nationwide transform their lives, bank accounts, and
law practices into successful, revenue producing businesses.

Starting in 2009 with the growth of myDUIattorney.org from scratch into a nationwide advertiser for DUI attorneys, Richard now helps hundreds of solo practitioners, and small law firms of 2 to 20 attorneys in 17 different practice areas (including Family Law, Personal Injury, Criminal Defense, Immigration and more) learn, implement, and profit from sound marketing that law school dares not teach.

If you're ready to improve your law practice and break free of mediocrity & struggle, contact Richard today at Jacobs & Whitehall.

www.jacobsandwhitehall.com

(888) 570-7338

TABLE OF CONTENTS

What's Changed (2013-2022) In Attorney Marketing

Welcome back to **Secrets of Attorney Marketing Law School Dares Not Teach**, 3rd edition. It has been thoroughly revised, expanded, and updated for 2022 and beyond. Because the first edition came out in 2013, many attorneys want to know what has changed in the attorney marketing world between then and now, and what is going to happen in the future – and I'm going to address that here.

Here's what has NOT changed: Clients still need legal help. They still need qualified, highly experienced attorneys to help them with their legal situations. Clients' behavior in handling their legal situations has not changed, just as human nature has not changed over thousands of years.

There are still people procrastinating until the day before their arraignment, until they've been beaten by their spouse for the 50th time (domestic violence), until their parent is in hospice, days from death (to create an estate plan) before they will call your office.

Then there are the proactive people that react immediately to their situation by searching for and retaining a lawyer within a day.

The third type of person takes their time to decide, needing to: pray on it, sleep on it, think on it, talk to their wife or husband, or weigh their options for days, weeks, or months. None of these customer archetypes have changed, because people do not change, even though technology does.

Here's what HAS changed: As I am sure you know by looking around, people spend much of their time with bent neck, a smartphone in their hand, and their eyes glued to the screen. Living examples of Darwinism are walking into traffic, getting hit by cars. They're walking off cliffs and dying while playing Pokémon Go or texting.

Some call them *smombies* (smartphone zombies). What I'm seeing, as undoubtedly you are, is the rapid proliferation and use of mobile phones and tablets all day and night, in every situation, social or otherwise.

In 2013, website visitors came mostly from laptops and desktops. Perhaps 20% or less came from smartphones and tablets. In 2021, the numbers had nearly switched. At the end of 2021, mobile website visitors were 80% and rising. They are poised to top out at 90% in 2022, possibly even more.

Laptops and desktops will not disappear by any means, but mobile devices' use now outpaces their use, and will continue to widen its lead into 2022.

In fact, 90% of Facebook users access, post, comment, read, and interact from their mobile device. Mobile devices have achieved record market penetration and widespread use.

What's the consequence of these trends and facts when it comes to your law firm's success and growth?

1. Focus <u>first</u> on how your website and your online presence appear on mobile devices. THEN, look at how they appear on a laptop or desktop. This is a major shift in thinking, but thankfully, all good marketing principles still apply. It's no longer enough to design your website, your landing pages, your AVVO, Google+, Yelp, or Attorney Website Bio page using your laptop – you must now accommodate what a desktop sees, what an iPad sees, what a smartphone sees in both vertical and landscape format, and what different web browsers see – sometimes even what an app sees.

2. <u>Google (and YouTube</u>, which Google owns) are the predominant way people search for information on the web (over 80% of searchers use Google, and with YouTube combined, it's closer to 90%).

3. <u>Google Maps (Google+), Yelp, & AVVO</u> have become highly trusted for their fair review process. Google+, Yelp, AVVO, and your website are the top four places where you <u>must get</u> as many good reviews as it takes (and each market and metro is different) to compete with your

fellow lawyers. Reviews, testimonials and case studies are becoming more trusted and relied upon by potentials when considering whom to hire.

4. Potential clients can research and compare multiple lawyers faster and easier than ever using the internet. Web-enabled smartphones are omnipresent, so it is more important than ever to stand out and differentiate yourself from your competitors.

Within half a second (literally), a Google search from your smartphone will display 10+ attorneys for a given practice area and metro.

If someone chooses to visit your website amidst the distraction and multiplicity of choices; if a potential client starts reading your articles or engaging with your web presence, ANY distraction can pull away their attention – a Facebook update, phone call from their wife, text from a friend, competing ads, and more.

All these things feed the distracted mind and can make people leave your website and break their attorney-seeking pattern. Who knows when they'll remember to start searching again, and will your website be the one they remember? Highly doubtful. Beware: distractions. are worse than ever and conspiring to rob you and your potential clients of their attention at every turn.

Other than these issues, there are other questions that I have received over the years that were not addressed in the first version.

Q: "Rich, my practice area is XYZ, it seems that you talk about criminal defense, family law and other practice areas, but what about mine? Mine is different."

I've successfully marketing attorneys in over twenty (20) practice areas and have yet to see an area of law that needs to be marketed differently or one that does not work with fundamental marketing principles.

No matter how specialized or unusual your area of law is, if it is B2B or B2C, if it is long-term or short-term, the same marketing principles apply regardless. Undoubtedly, these principles will continue to work well into the future.

The only difference I have ever seen in marketing, whether it is to corporations or individuals, is this: There are short-term immediate legal problems such as being arrested, making bail, or having an imminent court date. Then there are long-term legal problems such as considering a divorce, filing bankruptcy, filing a civil suit or personal injury case.

**There are only two types of legal problems:
short-term and long-term.**

Not everyone is going to have to respond to their legal issue the same day they see your advertisement or visit your website. That's why you MUST follow up with unconverted clients.

Follow up is more important than ever, especially in light of all the distractions and options in today's world.

Remember, it does not matter what practice area you are in, the marketing is the same. The only difference is short-term versus long-term legal problems.

People tend to respond to legal problems in three predictable ways regardless of the practice area:

[1] The first group, as soon as they sense a legal problem or one arises, want to immediately jump on it and hire an attorney so they can have peace of mind. These are great clients, but these are the clients that everyone thinks are the only kind that are out there.

[2] The second group takes days, weeks or even months to decide. They need to sleep on it, think about it, mull it over, pray on it, talk with family, and torture themselves with the decision for a period of time before they decide. These are the people that require consistent, informative, and non-spammy or non-annoying follow-ups to get them over the hump to hire you. There is nothing wrong with these clients. They make good clients, but just take time to make a decision.

[3] The third group of people are procrastinators, avoiders, the head in the sand, the "I will do anything except hire a lawyer for my case until I have to" types of people. These people wait until the night before a court date or the day before the statute of limitations expires to seek legal counsel. They can be good clients but, they too need consistent follow-up and prodding to get them to act.

All three groups above can become your clients. All three types of client behavior must be understood and marketed to properly to get them to retain you.

With all this in mind, please enjoy this book. Check out new chapters on: Live Chat, Social Media, Advanced Strategies for Obtaining Reviews, Advance Price-Defense Strategy, and more.

I think you will find the 2022 edition even more informative, helpful and useful to growing your law practice and succeeding in today's world.

A toast to your success!

Introduction: I Still Didn't Write This Book…

I have a confession to make. I didn't write a single word of this book back in 2013, and I STILL didn't write the updates for the 3rd edition you are now reading.

I didn't have a ghostwriter nor did I write it myself so how is that possible?

I spoke the content instead. I sat in front of my computer, used summary notes, spoke to the screen, recorded my voice, and had it transcribed. I then edited, taking out the "um's", and the "uh's", and corrected the grammar of my spoken sentences. That's how I spoke, not wrote this book.

Later I'll show you how and why 'speaking a book' (as opposed to "old fashioned writing") is a profitable breakthrough you can use in **your own law practice**.

Background: Richard Jacobs, Attorney Marketing Expert with Speakeasy Marketing, Inc.

So who am I, and why did I speak this book? Why should you read or believe anything I have to say? My name is Richard Jacobs, and I've been doing online and offline marketing for criminal defense attorneys for the past 7 years.

As you can see by the testimonials in this book, I know what I am doing. I've gotten real results for real attorneys. Anyone reading is welcome to call these guys and gals and ask about my work. They'll give you an honest assessment.

How did I get into the legal field, consulting with attorneys when I am not an attorney myself? Here's my history:

One night, seven years ago, I was surfing the web, and I decided to look up the most expensive Google Adwords keywords. I learned "DUI lawyer" and "mesothelioma lawyer" cost as much as $100 per click!

I figured, "Hmm, this is a market that should have some money in it because it looks like people are spending a whole heck of a lot on advertising."

I wondered, "Do I want to deal with attorneys? They can be kind of a mean, scary bunch!"

In the end, I deliberately chose to throw myself into it; not only for the potential money, but for the challenge.

My thinking at the time was: If I can use SEO (search engine optimization) to be number 1 in Google for terms like "Los Angeles DUI lawyer" or "New York DWI attorney"- and not have to pay $100 per click that some lawyers appeared to be paying, then I should be able to help a lot of attorneys without breaking their bank accounts.

I then started myDuiAttorney.org, providing advertising to attorneys nationwide to help them get DUI / DWI leads.

The site started with zero visitors. After 18 months, from scratch, I built it up to well approximately 1,100 visitors a day from Google. At its peak, I had 120 attorney clients, all receiving DUI / DWI leads nationwide.

After doing that for a while, I grew discouraged. I realized I was a one trick pony. While some lawyers were great at converting my leads into clients, others had a tough time converting ANY leads. Leads would also frequently go dry in various metros for 2 weeks or more. Some lawyers would get scared and quit the service.

Because I was simply a lead provider and viewed as a utility like cable television, the only time clients contacted me was to complain or quit. I decided I didn't want to operate that way. I wanted to work more closely with attorneys and help them market their practice in a diversified way – SEO, getting more reviews on AVVO, Google+, Yelp, sending a newsletter to past client to stimulate referrals, and more.

I decided to cannibalize that entire business and sold the website. I then started Speakeasy Marketing, Inc. and now provide full-service, diversified, done-for-you marketing for attorneys in over 20 practice areas, from Family Law to Personal Injury, to Criminal Defense, and more. I also have a much closer relationship with my clients, and happier, more successful ones to boot.

Additionally, since my team has grown to over 22 support staff, we spend a lot of time testing and evaluating what's working and what's not, talking with lawyers in major metros throughout the United States in many different practice areas, and honing our skills to provide the best marketing we can.

Some of the topics you're going to learn more about to help improve your marketing come from my best ideas:

SEO (Search Engine Optimization)

Why ranking on the first page of Google for a few commercial keywords won't produce great results (and what <u>DOES</u> produce results, instead). The 3 pillars of white-hat, proper SEO that will get you calls from real clients with money.

Direct mail

Called "jailer mailer" in some states and metros. Myths and misconceptions about the types of clients it attracts, how much it costs, and more.

Authoring A Practice-Area Guide For Potential Clients

Authoring a book used to take years of writing and editing and can now be done in 30 days, for a fraction of the effort.

Why write a book such as: "Surviving divorce in Los Angeles" or "What's The Value of Your Auto Accident Case?"? Because being one of the few attorney authors in your metro and practice area(s) will increase your authority celebrity, and expertise in the eyes and minds of potentials.

This, of course, leads to fewer clients that hire your competitors, and more that retain YOU.

Google Adwords (aka Google Pay Per Click)

Does it really work? Can it be made profitable? Why is it so darn expensive and how can it be made to produce a 3:1 or 5:1 ROI?

Getting More Referrals From Past Clients Consistently

Why Christmas and Birthday cards aren't enough to stimulate consistent, profitable referrals and what to do about it. Since referrals are claimed to be the best clients, and often pre-sold on your services, why aren't you paying attention to this marketing method more? Here's what to do and how.

How to Build a Mobile-Friendly, Client Attracting (Instead of a Client-Repelling) Website

How do you build an effective website that gets people interested in your representation and compels them to call?

Why do some websites attract tons of traffic but get zero calls while others are a source of multiple leads per week?

Instead of visiting your website and clicking away to a competitor's website, I'll show you how to get potentials engage with your articles, pre-sold on you as their attorney, and calling you for that all-important initial consult.

Testing and Tracking of All Your Marketing

What can be tracked, can be improved and made to turn an ROI. What is not tracked becomes a source of worry ("I don't think it's working", "It feels like I'm getting more cases") and careless spending of marketing dollars.

How To Avoid A Hostage Situation
With Bad Attorney Marketing Vendors

How do you spot bad actors who want your money and will provide poor or no results in return? How can you ensure that you own your website, its content, your reviews, and your entire online presence, not RENT it from a marketing company?

There's a lot more that we're going to cover in this revised 3rd edition of "Secrets of Attorney Marketing Law School Dares Not Teach".

With all of this in mind, welcome inside this book. You'll likely find it contains contrarian, massively useful, straight to the point, eye-opening, profitable marketing strategies and tactics that will grow your practice more than even before.

…Now open your mind and let's begin:

FORGET PROFESSIONALISM – HAVING AN OPEN MIND

I'm not afraid to tell you every detail of how I help attorneys market their practice, and you will soon see that I'm not kidding either. Why am I not afraid? Don't I have "trade secrets" to protect?

I am not worried about competition, nor am I worried about you knowing all my secrets.

Unfortunately, 95% of readers of this book, maybe even more, are not going to do anything I tell them in this book.

So why not tell you everything, without fear, for the benefit of the few that will take action, implement, and profit?

Since I'm not afraid to "reveal all", you, in turn, must keep an open mind while reading this book. Don't get hung up on thoughts such as, "That's not professional," or "People don't read nowadays." These assumptions hold you back and close your mind off to what's possible and will limit your success.

Don't let anyone's opinion stop you from trying a particular method of marketing; real-world experience should be your guide, not fear and worrying about what your colleagues think. After all, who pays your mortgage?

Your gut reaction to a particular marketing method may be, "Oh, direct mail, that's unprofessional. I feel like I am hounding people by doing that." Or you might think, "Pay-per-click? It's a scam. I would _never_ do that."

Open your mind and try these things. If not, you're going to remain where you are; fighting every month to cover your monthly nut and not getting ahead of the game.

...and if you DO harness your marketing, implement various marketing methods and course-correct along the way? You can make well beyond what you are making now.

If you want to make $400k+ as a criminal defense lawyer, if you want to break the $1 million mark as an injury lawyer, if you want to have a successful bankruptcy practice instead of contemplating bankruptcy, then your mantra must be: "How CAN I do XYZ?" instead of "I can't".

Success and a healthy, wealthy practice means you must be involved in your marketing, even if it is completely done for you. Marketing must be a critical part of your practice. Even a small degree of involvement with a good vendor who implements for you, will allow you to focus on what you do best: providing legal representation to clients in need.

If you're willing to have an open mind, continue reading. If not, put this book down or close out the screen and don't read any further.

YOU MAY HARBOR ASSUMPTIONS YOU DON'T EVEN KNOW YOU HAVE

As an attorney you're probably great at digging deep and uprooting assumptions in a client's case to help them win. It's the heart of what makes you a good attorney. However, when it comes to marketing your practice effectively, the assumptions we all have can end up hurting us.

Here are several <u>poisonous assumptions</u> I hear often:

"My clients are different. They are sophisticated, white collar people who wouldn't respond to this kind of marketing."

"My clients are different. They are unsophisticated, blue collar folks who don't read. They don't have patience for this kind of stuff."

"Direct mail is unethical. I don't want to do it. You only get cheapskate tire-kickers, anyway."

"My competitor, Joe Smith, Esq., is at the top of page on Google for 'Timbuktu Immigration Lawyer,' or 'Dallas Worker's Compensation Attorney', so he must be doing really well. If I could just get above him in Google, THAT would solve all my problems."

"I've been a lawyer for 25 years. Don't you think I've tried it all before? SEO doesn't work. Newsletters don't work. XYZ doesn't work."

"The economy is really bad. People have no money. That's just how it is in my metro / in my practice area."

"Everyone's on a payment plan. No one has money to pay. In this economy people are barely surviving as it is, so how can I afford to do marketing?"

Once your mind accepts poisonous assumptions as true, it throws a wet blanket over your ability to market. These assumptions are pure poison. Watch out if you start to think them or similar negative thoughts.

Here is some of the non-traditional marketing we've tried that has succeeded:

We provided custom coasters, matchbooks, wristbands and napkins with a call to action of "Call (800) 555-5555 if you are arrested for a DUI!" I had an agreement with 50+ bars around the country that would hand them out or place them beneath customers' drinks because we provided these items for free.

Although our attorney clients didn't get a ton of calls, people did call that were actually arrested for DUI and some of our clients were hired and paid for representation because of the advertising.

Would you imagine such a way of advertising would work? It goes to show, you can't know until you try.

We've tried direct mail to people in foreclosure, to people arrested for crimes, to people arrested for DUI, to people injured in an accident.

One mailer was a crumpled letter inside a mini trash can, offering legal assistance.

Guess what? This mailer, although the attorney resisted in the beginning, generated a lot of calls from potentials – some of whom became clients of my attorney (and paid him!). Why?

Because it was crazy and unique to receive a trash can in the mail, vs. a boring letter inside a boring, white envelope, with the same boring gobbledygook every other attorney sends.

We've also emailed 10,000+ website visitors, using a 7-part email follow up series. Once someone fills in a form on the web to request help with their legal situation, the email series automatically emailed the potential client a follow up email every 3rd day, for 21 days.

Each email explained some aspect of their case and educated the potential client (the emails were not sales pitches). After reading 2 or 3 emails, people called back on their own, and ended up hiring our attorney clients more often.

What Other Non-Traditional Marketing Have We Tried?

We've interviewed nearly 700 attorneys over Skype and by phone, asked them legal questions and answers about their practice area(s), recorded, transcribed, and edited those answers into articles for their websites, and help them earn several thousand additional clients they otherwise would never have attracted.

We then made YouTube® videos from the same interview content and placed those videos both on YouTube® and on their websites.

These videos weren't professional looking and frankly some were downright grainy. However, none were the typical, stand in front of your law books, tell the world how great you are type of video. What they did do was educated potential clients who were searching for legal help, and inspired them to call the attorney for an initial consult.

Guess what? It got the attorneys paying clients. People saw the videos and saw these were real people, not just websites with text on them. Potentials picked up the phone, called the attorney's office and mentioned the videos!

Would you rather spend $10,000 with a "professional video crew" make 1 or 2 commercials for YouTube, or create a series of educational videos that answer potentials' questions, make them comfortable with you, and get them to call for a consult?

For one client, we did a series of free 24-hour recorded messages that led to an 800 number potential clients called. It had prerecorded information on fighting Criminal charges and a prompt at the end of the message to 'press 1 to connect to the attorney'.

It worked, because a free recorded message is a non-threatening way to get information on your legal case, and to call the attorney if they wished. Getting non-threatening information, without being pitched, puts people at ease, builds trust, positions you as the expert, and helps them to engage with you.

Which one of these strategies made you assume "That would never work!", "It makes me uncomfortable", "That's unprofessional", or "MY clients are different and would never respond to that kind of marketing"?

Assumptions like these do nothing to make you more money or attract more clients. All they do is hurt you and prevent you from succeeding. Cast them off and <u>try.</u>

I wouldn't write a book if such marketing didn't work. I wouldn't have testimonials if they didn't work. I wouldn't waste years of my life doing this if they didn't work. Open your litigious mind and let's move forward.

Countless Reasons to Treat Potential, Current, & Past Clients Like GOLD (Orchestrating Their Experience)

Why should you make extra special effort to treat your potential clients, current clients and past clients as good as gold?

I've marketed for, talked to, and mystery shopped hundreds of law firms. Some attorneys are amazing at converting potential clients into  paying clients. These "superhumans" retain 1 in 3 that call.

Other firms are dying and couldn't retain a potential client if you stapled them to their arm. These guys barely retain one in every 50 that call!

The reasons why are not the reasons you think.

This is a new take on an old, "Golden Rule"... One of the biggest factors of an lawyer's success is how they and their firm (if they have partners) treat everyone they interact with.

People call law offices for all sorts of different reasons. It may be someone calling with just a clarifying question or someone who is calling on their case and need serious help.

There are calls from people that just retained you – they're doing a reality check to combat their buyer's remorse and make sure they made the right decision. Then there are calls are from people whose case has just finished. They are likely in the process of becoming a past client and are at the height of their gratitude or disappointment with you.

Finally, old clients / past clients may be calling for new help, to refer, or with questions.

Why it is so important to treat every caller like GOLD, even if they seem to be a tire kicker or not truly interest or even tell you "no"? Treating people well doesn't any money, and it doesn't take much effort, but <u>the results can be amazing</u>.

One attorney who does this successfully is my oldest client, Kevin Leckerman, Esq. Kevin focuses on DUI / DWI Defense in Philadelphia and southern New Jersey. He has listened to what I've told him to do for the past 7 years, and he practices what's preached here.

Kevin went reviewed his entire sales process and is treating his clients better and better. No, he's not sucking up to them, telling them what they want to hear. He's treating with respect and communicating often at every stage of their interaction with him.

Kevin's Case Study:

Kevin had 20 fewer clients last year than the year before and STILL made the same amount of money. He spent more time with each client, allowing him to analyze their cases 100 ways to Sunday, and represent them to the absolute fullest.

Because he had fewer clients, he spent more time with each. Clients were much happier and <u>he achieved more wins and overall better results on most of his cases</u>.

Because clients were happier, they willingly gave him more positive reviews on AVVO, Google+, Yelp and on his website, which attracted more clients in a virtuous cycle.

Emotionally, he felt great because he had a much higher "win percentage", and he wasn't running back and forth to court as often, making appearances, onboarding new clients, answering questions, and babysitting poor clients.

A critical element of his success was that Kevin doubled his fees, which kept his income at the same level.

Kevin and I recently talked about all the benefits we've seen come from treating everyone like gold. When we were done, we were both amazed at the list of "benefits".

We built the list by going over why and how you should treat people well at every stage of their interaction with you and your firm.

I wrote the following from the perspective of a potential, current or past client:

Step #1: <u>Before I've Retained You</u> If you treat me well and give me a great experience, I am less likely to no-show appointments. This is because I am more comfortable with you. I can tell you're listening to me and not coming across as arrogant or judgmental.

I am less likely to tell you that I don't have any money or that you are "too expensive" just to blow you off for another lawyer who treats me better.

I am less likely to avoid your follow-up calls after I tell you, "I have to think it over. I'm not ready to hire you just yet."

I am less likely to have mixed feelings about hiring you, making me easy prey for low fee, grind mill attorneys competing with you who provide bare bones representation.

I am less likely to shut down, stop listening and not believe what you tell me or think: "You only want my money and don't care about me as a person."

Step #2: <u>Once I Have Retained You & Become Your Client</u>
I am less likely to have buyer's remorse or feel like a fool when I tell my friends and family that I hired you, only to

have them say, "Why did you hire *that guy* when your Uncle Bob is a lawyer? He can help you and you shouldn't waste money on this guy."

If you treat me well and give me a great experience, I am less likely to stop making payments on a payment plan you graciously offer me, even though I know the judge will not let you withdraw from my case.

I am less likely to unintentionally do things to hurt my ongoing case because I don't truly trust you, making me take matters into my own hands.

I am less likely to suffer sleepless nights and constantly worry about my case, causing me to become an emotional drain on you and your admins with my incessant questions.

I am less likely to think you are my psychologist, rather than my attorney.

Step #3: <u>Once You Have Resolved My Case And I'm Now A Past Client</u>, if you thanked me for my business and keep up with me periodically after my case, I am more likely to remember your name and refer you to my friends and family if they have legal troubles now or in the future.

I am more likely to spontaneously, or especially if asked, give you a good testimonial that you can use on your website to help obtain more clients for years to come.

I am more likely to think back on my experience with you as positive and always remember you as the "White Knight" that saved me. I am more likely to call you first rather than turn to Google if I have a future legal problem.

Are you impressed with this laundry list of benefits? Kevin and I sure were when we realized this!

There's a preponderance of positives that happen if you treat your potential, current and past clients like gold at every step of your legal representation of them.

"Little touches" can as simple as candies, a handwritten thank you note, always being pleasant on the phone, returning phone calls promptly.

Then there is the "big touch" which, of course, is defending each client to the absolute best of your abilities – as if their case was the most important case you've ever worked on.

Getting 'Enough' Reviews: Why Third Party Reviews Are Now Vital To Your Success

In 2022 and beyond, third party reviews on the internet have become vital to succeeding and competing in your metro and practice area(s).

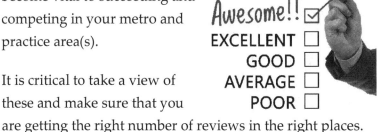

It is critical to take a view of these and make sure that you are getting the right number of reviews in the right places.

Imagine pulling out your smartphone and Googling 'Mexican Restaurants'. See Lupita's with 84, 3 ½ star reviews? Compare it to Alejandro's with 400, 4 ½ star reviews, and tell me…

which Mexican restaurant would *you* choose?

More like than not you'll choose the one with more reviews that has a higher average review rating.

The same thing happens when you go to Amazon dot com.

Amazon is wonderful because there are reviews for almost every product. I find myself choosing the products with the most reviews just like my father used Consumer Reports® to make decisions.

In today's smart phone everywhere world, <u>people rely heavily</u> on AVVO, Google+, Yelp reviews and reviews on your own law firm's website.

Sounds great, but it's not easy to get reviews – in fact, it's quite difficult and time consuming to get them.

Many lawyers have a defeatist attitude when it comes to getting reviews:

> "I provide criminal defense. No one is going to want to have their name attached to a review."

> "I ask my clients, but they never do it.
> I don't want to annoy them."

> "My clients are unsophisticated and
> don't use computers very much."

Sure, there's merit and genuine concern about these arguments, but at this very moment, criminal defense attorneys, tax attorneys, family law attorneys, and every practice area you can think of, in every metro in the United States have tons of website, Google+, Yelp, and AVVO 10.0 reviews. Do they have magical or more agreeable clients?

How do some attorneys earn dozens of 5-star Google+ and Yelp reviews, when you can't seem to get any of your clients to review you?

If John Smith's clients has dozens of reviews, it means that <u>your clients will review you</u> if they are asked in the right way.

(unless you are truly a bad attorney, but bad attorneys would never even read this book, so you're a good one)

Don't think clients will be too embarrassed to post their review because a lot of them will, regardless of what happened in their case.

Another tip: when a review is posted, it does not have to give private details of a client's case. It can be subtle enough where the person's privacy is still protected. You may have to tell clients that they don't have to discuss the specifics of their case in a review. They can leave out critical details that they feel would embarrass them. That's totally fine. Here's an example:

"Attorney John Smith went to court five times to file motions to help me in my case. I was surprised as his level of dedication and the massive amount of hard work he put into my case. Thank you so much, Mr. Smith!" – Amy S.

Additionally, on some platforms your client doesn't have to put their actual picture or full name. This is possible on Google+, on Yelp, on AVVO, and especially on your website.

If your client feels like they will be embarrassed, they can change their profile name and picture so their privacy is protected. It's perfectly acceptable.

Getting "Enough" Reviews

The threshold of "enough reviews" is surprisingly low in many metros and practice areas.

Approximately 80% of the metros and practice have attorneys with top rankings in Google+ and Yelp with 5, 5-star reviews or less. (although this number is growing)

This means that 6, 7 or 10 reviews over a year's time is an achievable goal.

Look at it this way: you're going to be in practice for ten, twenty or even thirty more years. The work you do in the next year will serve you well for a long time.

Consistently working at accumulating reviews over the next 12 months is a great investment of your time and effort.

It gets even better once you reach 10, 20, or 30 reviews, because puts you at the top of a mountain in an unassailable position because of all the reviews you have.

Other attorneys will look at you and sigh, "How did he/she get so many reviews? I can never do that", and give up before they even start.

You want to get enough reviews to DAUNT your competitors into giving up before they start. This only further strengthens your positioning.

Although getting reviews usually takes a solid year, sometimes a few months more, it's worth it. Reviews are extremely powerful and they are relied upon very heavily by potential clients in making their decision of whom to hire.

"What if you get a bad review?"

Very few people have a perfectly clean record online. I've spoken to many lawyers who have one or more bad reviews, yet their practices are thriving.

How is this possible?

Unfortunately, you can't prevent people from leaving a bad review. On occasion, you'll have a client who is impossible to make happy, no matter how much effort you put into their case.

I've heard of clients getting $200,000 settlements that complain it wasn't enough. One of my Criminal Defense Attorney clients helped someone get a reduced sentence of 13 months instead of 9 years and got a bad review. Imagine that!

Since living in fear of a bad review, or not trying to get good reviews is <u>not going to prevent</u> the occasional bad review, here's what you need to do:

Consistently accumulate GOOD reviews from your happy clients to put the occasional bad review in context. Think about how you'd feel: You need a divorce lawyer, and you see the following:

Attorney1:   (1 bad review, zero good reviews)

Attorney2:   (2 bad reviews, 12 good reviews)

Which attorney are you more likely to hire?

The one with more bad reviews, BECAUSE… that attorney also has 12 GOOD reviews, which make the bad reviews seem… not so bad.

Let's look at Amazon. Did you know – nearly ZERO products on Amazon have 100% positive reviews?

Amazon's rating system is from 1 to 5 stars. It's hard to find a product that doesn't have several 1, 2, 3, 4 and 5 star reviews.

Consumers not only expect, but understand that no product or service is going to have all positive reviews. If you live in fear of getting a bad review, the day you DO get a bad review (and you will, statistically), you won't have any good reviews to offset it, and you'll have to make a mad dash to quickly get good reviews to counteract the bad one.

"What are the best websites to get reviews on?"

There are hundreds of websites that allow for reviews, but the great news is, there are currently only a few websites that are vital to get reviews on in 2022:

1) Your own website

2) Avvo.com

3) Yelp

4) Google Maps (Google+)

These are the four most important places for you to have positive reviews, because they are looked at most often by potential clients, and all four of these websites rank at the top of Google search for many, many keywords.

Other websites like Thumbtack.com or local review sites are not important and they do not show up strongly in Google search results. Focus your attention and get reviews where they count – forget the other 500 websites – they won't help you much at all.

Great news: you have 100% control over your own website. You can choose which reviews to highlight, how they are displayed, in what order, and on which pages of your site. If you need more reviews on your website, you can always repurpose and rewrite reviews from Google+, Yelp and AVVO (so long as the intent of the review isn't changed. You may also want to ask permission of the reviewer to do so, but that's up to you).

Here's how to make the review-getting process simpler for the websites you DON'T control (Google+, Yelp, AVVO):

When asking for a review, ask your client which service they commonly use and which is easiest for them. Do they use Yelp? Do they have a Gmail account? Do they use Avvo?

Whatever website is most comfortable for them is the website on which you should ask them to review you; NOT the website YOU want them to use.

What's easiest for your client is what's most likely to be used

Google+ (Google Maps) – ask your client if they use Gmail. For people who do, it's easy to write a review, especially when using their smartphone. Note: clients should not create a Gmail account just for the purpose of writing one review and never used again. Google will see that there is no activity on the account except this review and they will not post it.

Yelp – Yelp will suppress a client's review unless they've previously reviewed two or more other businesses on Yelp. If your review will be the first, ask the client to please review their local movie theatre, hairdresser, florist, coffee shop, or other service provider so your review doesn't get hidden.

AVVO – AVVO is easier than Yelp or Google+ to post a review, and should be a backup option.

Your Website – If your client isn't computer-savvy, they can email their review, or even hand write a review you can scan and post on your website. Reviews on your website should also be a backup option, but remember you can re-purpose reviews on Yelp, Google+ and AVVO, having a review perform "double duty".

The moral of the review-getting story?

Get reviews however you can. Get them in the easiest way for your clients. Do not force someone to do a certain way just because *you want* a certain type of review.

Genuine vs. Faked Reviews:

Reviews should never be faked. Do you want to incur the wrath of your state or local bar association? Negative attention and a blackmail situation from competitors? Possible disciplinary action or even disbarment? The attention of the attorney general in your state?

In New York State, a few years ago, the Attorney General issued a crackdown on fake reviews, and many businesses were laid waste by the negative press and legal fallout.

No matter how desperate you are, never fake reviews. It's never worth it.

Can my clients use my office computer to post reviews?

Never have clients use your office computers or your smartphone to post reviews. Google, Yelp and other services track the IP address of the reviewer and they track past usage on a particular computer and accounts associated with that computer or device.

If you try to have clients use your computers or your phone to review your firm, it will not work after the first review, and nearly all of your reviews will be hidden.

Great Tips For Getting More Reviews

Did you know that reviews can come from past clients as well as current clients? There's no reason not to ask a current client at various stages, milestones or watershed moments in their case for a positive review.

The smart attorneys get reviews even before their client's case is over. Doing so makes the client believe in you more and makes them happier with their result, strangely enough.

Since they've gone to the trouble to write a positive review, they automatically feel more invested in you. To feel negative about you or change their main after a client has written a positive review would create "cognitive dissonance", nearly regardless of the result you get them.

By giving you a positive review, a client publicly displays their feelings, making it hard to change them later on.

Besides current or past clients, attorneys who are friends or associates of yours can post positive reviews!

Let's say you're Attorney Bob Smith and I'm Attorney Alice Jones. My review could say, *"I've known Attorney Bob Smith for 15 years. We practiced in the same courts in central Texas. I found Attorney Bob Smith to be a zealous advocate for his clients. I see the good work that he does and if I had a client with the legal situation that fit his practice areas, I would recommend him in a heartbeat"*.

There is nothing wrong with that review.

The review is honest and it came from another attorney. So what? It is not saying that he or she is a client. It discloses exactly the nature of the review and why those reviews are perfectly acceptable for any platform.

This is a great way to get you more reviews, putting you on the path to getting "enough reviews".

...how many reviews are "enough"?

One benchmark is your competition's websites, Google Maps Yelp and Avvo review levels.

How many reviews do your top-ranked local competitors have?

Often (but not always), getting just 3-4 more reviews than all your competitors on a given platform are enough.

You don't need to go crazy and get hundreds of reviews like a restaurant or a hotel. Surprisingly, the number of reviews your competitors have is quite low in many metros.

Holmes, Diggs, Eames & Sadler
4.8 ★★★★★ (5) · Divorce Lawyer

Ramos Law Group, PLLC
4.3 ★★★★★ (23) · Divorce Lawyer

Cynthia Tracy, Attorney at Law, P.C.
1 review · Divorce Lawyer

Another watershed that's important is the 5 or more, 5-star review level on Google Maps. Once you get five positive reviews, several gold stars will appear next to your listing which makes it stand out and draw more attention from surfers.

Consider it your first hurdle when accumulating reviews on Google+ (and Yelp).

On Yelp, 5 positive reviews is the ante to the game, even though you may not get gold stars next to your name. On Yelp, If you someone comments on your review, saying it's: funny or useful, or if a power Yelp reviewer reviews you, this helps your review rank better.

If the reviewer posts a picture of you, your law firm or anything related with their review, this also strengthens your reviews ranking power.

Powerful Reviews Are Detailed Reviews

Without violating someone's privacy, the more detail your reviews have, the better. For example, if someone says, "I like Attorney Jane Doe. She really helped me out and she did a wonderful job on my case," it's mediocre, but ok.

Here, instead, is an informative, useful, compelling, and specific testimonial:

"I was pulled over on suspicion of DUI. I was breath-tested and they took my license. Attorney Jane Doe went to court for me 7 times and got my breath test results suppressed. I was facing 30 days in jail and she got me zero jail time - just probation. Thank you so much, Attorney Jane Doe!"

Regardless of your practice area(s), what makes a good testimonial is the same: family law, for estate planning, criminal defense, patent law, immigration, etc.

Want to make your reviews even more powerful? Ask your client to put one or two keywords in their review. Warning: you don't want to stuff the testimonial full of different  keywords like "San Diego Family Lawyer", "Divorce Lawyer of San Diego". However, it helps if those words appear once in a testimonial because Google, Yelp and Avvo all consider keywords to be important in making a review powerful.

Overcoming Client's Laziness and Fear:

Yes, people are lazy. Yes, people need to be reminded multiple times to post a review. However, if you stick to this activity for a year or more, you'll be surprised at how many reviews you can accumulate. Once you start getting calls from potential clients who mention your reviews – and once those potential clients start hiring you easily, you will see the power of positive reviews.

Advanced use of reviews for maximum effect:

Let's say you practice family law and you've been smart enough to accumulate reviews for contested divorce, uncontested divorce, child custody, child support, emergency removals, and more.

Put your child custody-related reviews on pages of your website that have articles talking about child custody.

Put alimony and spousal maintenance-related reviews on pages of your website that talk about that subject. Match the review type to the content of the article on that page.

Here's why: When I search for legal help, not only do I want answers to my questions, but I want to know that you, the attorney, have handled cases that are similar to my case.

I think my case is unique, but it may not be. If I see you have helped someone with a fact pattern just like my case, or someone who is the same age, gender, or circumstances, and you got a good result, I am far more likely to be swayed by a related, relevant review than a generic one.

That's how you can boost the effectiveness of your pre-existing reviews and get the most mileage out of new ones.

How about making an audio recording of your reviews in addition to only text? You can then place a still image on top of the audio and now it becomes a video you can post on YouTube®. Some potential clients would rather listen than read. This gives you more mileage out of the same review.

Your review video can also show your name, your website, phone number, and email. Of course, it would be even more powerful if you could get your client to do a video testimonial, but in the event you can't do that, text and a still image video are helpful and will boost potential client's confidence in hiring you.

Even voice over videos with still images make it appear as if your client went out of his or her way to endorse you beyond just a written review.

One Last Tip To Maximizing Reviews

Contact your past clients monthly and ask them for a review, even if it has been a year or more since you worked with them. People forget as time passes. People get lazy.

People may not be ready or willing to post a review now, but may be happy to do so once they've had some distance from the un-pleasantries of their case.

Next month, or three months from now, the same people that said no or wouldn't review you may now do so.

A good way to periodically request reviews is to send out a monthly newsletter and to request reviews in the newsletter. You'll be surprised the number of people that will come out of the woodwork to review you.

Remember: asking people once a month is NOT bugging them – yes, some will complain, but that's going to happen no matter how infrequently you ask for reviews. Don't let it dissuade you from asking and getting the reviews you need to dominate your competition and attract more clients.

WHY PROPER TRACKING OF YOUR MARKETING MEANS SUCCESS VS. FAILURE

Individually tracking and testing each type of marketing you do is essential, especially in 2022 and beyond. Here's why: the answer can be found in a  famous quote from John Wanamaker, the first retailer to place a half-page newspaper ad in 1874. His famous quote is: "Half of my advertising/marketing is wasted, but I don't know which half."

Don't be a Wanamaker and waste thousands of dollars a month in misguided and non-optimized marketing (*thousands of dollars a month is no exaggeration*) with case values in the neighborhood of: $1,200 for bankruptcy; $2,000 DUI; $10,000 personal injury; $4,000 family law; $5,000 estate planning, $1200 immigration.

Would you rather assume, hope, think or feel like your marketing is working? Smart lawyers want fact and evidence-based marketing to show them ROI (or not). If you were an average attorney, you wouldn't be reading this book, and you certainly would not have read this far. Now let's keep going.

Worse than relying on gut instinct or feeling to make marketing decisions, not tracking each type of marketing you do will lead you to draw erroneous conclusions without the facts (and what court case can exist in the absence of facts?).

If you find yourself saying or thinking: "Google pay- per-click doesn't work", "Direct mail is expensive", "SEO takes too long", and other nebulous comments, then you're not tracking your marketing.

Attorneys that track their marketing say the following instead: "We're getting a 3 to 1 ROI on our Google Adwords ads", or "Direct mail was a breakeven, but it helped build our newsletter list and netted us 4 extra referrals in the past 12 months, so it had a 1.7 to 1 ROI", or "SEO took us 7 months to reach a breakeven point, and is now producing a 4 to 1 ROI, so after a year of doing it, we're running at a 1.35 to 1 ROI, but next year should be 3.5 to 1 or better because we'll have a full year of profitable SEO".

So how much does your SEO make you or cost you a month? How much money do you have to spend to get a potential to call you, then, based on your phone to hired client ratio, how much does it cost you to get a new client?

Even though you offer "free consultations" just like everyone else in your practice area, or a standard 33% of recovery, how much does it cost for you to get a client to retain you?

If you charge $2,500 for a case and it costs you $700 to retain a client, is that WORTH IT for you to do or is it unprofitable?

In working with over 700 attorneys the past seven years, <u>95% don't or won't track their marketing</u> – a serious problem.

Before we get into specific marketing tactics or strategies, whether social media, Google Adwords, newsletters, press releases, SEO, mobile marketing, and more… remember - unless you track your spend and results for each type of marketing you're doing, you will suffer poor or no returns.

"If you can't measure it, you can't improve it."
– Peter Drucker, management guru; author of best-selling management books.

This is why, once you start tracking each type of marketing you're doing individually, you can now test, tweak, and optimize each channel to boost your ROI, or turn a loser into a profitable winner.

Examples of "marketing channels" are: Yellow Pages, Google pay-per-click / adwords, search engine optimization of your website, YouTube videos, Live Chat, a newsletter to past clients, a magazine ad, a live speech to local prospects, and more. Each example is a marketing channel. Track each separately - root out the winners and losers - the money makers vs. the bloodsuckers.

In 2022, there's really no excuse not to do it, given that phone, email, and internet tracking is cheap and sophisticated.

You can track phone calls to your office from multiple phone numbers and locations. You can track potentials who complete a contact us form on your website. You can track walk-ins, revenue per case, per type of case, per associate, per day, per week, per month, and more. You can track anything under the sun for a few dollars a month in an automated way.

Don't tell me you ENJOY getting hounded by daily calls from marketing companies promising to "Get you on the 1st page of Google" or claiming that their service will "flood your website with new clients and produce a 10 to 1 ROI."

You know most of these claims are grossly optimistic, and more often, completely not true.

Still, you'd be surprised at how many attorneys try one form of marketing, then another, then another. Each time they're discouraged because it "didn't work", or "didn't seem to bring in enough clients".

Lawyers become serial marketing victims, spending $3000, $5000, even $10,000 a month with no clue if their marketing is producing new clients or a positive return on investment.

…and yes, marketing done properly, is an INVESTMENT.

Precious few attorneys have NOT been burned by marketers before. Either you or a colleague has spent thousands of dollars a month, only to realize the phone STILL doesn't ring.

Fool me once, shame on you.
Fool me twice, shame on me.
Replace Fear with Facts... TRACK!

My attorney clients, whether I bug them or they do it themselves, sleep well at night because they know they're not wasting money. If a marketing channel isn't making money, they know QUICKLY, and we then tweak it to profitability, or stop spending money on it, if it won't bring in new clients.

Another benefit? My attorney clients know, as their marketing consultant, if I am not doing my job. I can't BS my way out of it.

My attorney clients track their results, because I make them do it. I'm accountable for bringing them new leads and they are accountable for convincing those leads to retain them and pay their fees.

You work hard for your money. You must see where it's going and what it's doing.

What Does It Mean to Be Profitable? What Is ROI and Why Is It a True Measure of Results?

Thankfully, you'll find some marketing channels to be truly profitable, meaning they return 3 to 5 times your money or more (called return on investment, or 'ROI').

Even though this concept sounds like a no-brainer, there's more to it – keep reading.

Ex: Direct mail = 300% ROI;
        Google Adwords = 50% ROI;
        Yellow Pages = 20% ROI.
        SEO = 350% ROI.

Including paperwork, time spent going to and from court, office overhead, and other fees reduces your margin to 50% on any case you take.

Do you keep Yellow Pages? ($1.20 of YP revenue - $1 marketing – 50 cents margin = -30 cents). This means each Yellow Pages case you get LOSES you 30 cents on the dollar!

What 'looks' profitable may, in fact, be a loser.

Now imagine a broken change machine at a casino. You put in $20 and get back $100 change. Huh? You try the machine again with another $20 and it spits out $100 again.

How long and how fast are you going to feed this machine with twenties? As fast and as quietly as you can, because you're getting a 5:1 ROI on your money.

That is the power of a successful marketing channel that is tracked and is earning you a positive ROI – it's like a money machine you should want to feed as much as possible.

What do most attorneys do instead? They mistakenly complain: "SEO is expensive because I pay $1,500 a month. Yes, I'm getting cases, but I want to reduce my spend" or "sending a newsletter to my past clients cost $1.25 each – that's expensive and I don't think it's worth it".

Both are meaningless statements; the ROI you get from a give marketing channel is what <u>REALLY matters</u>.

Worse Yet – When Losers Drag Down Winners

Let's say you spend $5,000 a month on marketing in three different channels. Two are returning $8,000 a month, and the third is losing you $3,000 a month.

You spent $5,000 and took in $8,000 + $8,000 - $3,000 = $13,000. That's a 2.66x ROI right? (We're ignoring time in court and paperwork and admin salaries, i.e. "overhead")

This isn't a bad scenario – what's the problem here? Well, if you didn't track your marketing, this would be invisible to you, and you'd merrily go along, netting $13k revenue - $5k marketing spend = $8k a month, probably frustrated you're not making more.

Now what if you tracked and found the $3,000 loser?

Here's the magic of getting rid of the albatross around your neck and cutting out the loser:

You were spending $1,000 a month on the loser, so your monthly spend has decreased to $4,000.

$8k + $8k - $4k = $12k (vs $8k previously), **a $4,000 additional profit each and every month.**

You'd have to take on 2 additional cases a month to make this extra $4,000. Over a year, this would be 2 * 12 = 24 additional clients, wasting hundreds of hours of your time.

$4,000 per month additional profit * 12 months = **$48,000 a year increased profits – very doable and VERY profitable.**

Yes, it IS possible to increase your profits by $50,000 or more just because you started tracking, testing and tweaking your marketing.

Tracking frees you up to cut out true losers without any compunction or fear.

Let's take this even further to see what's possible...

How about doubling down on winners in addition to cutting out losers?

Maybe you are running local radio ads, yet you're afraid to increase your budget. Once tracked, you see that they're returning 3x what you spend.

Double down on that spend, (i.e. advertise in more markets, or add a morning drive time radio ad) and ride that winner!

It's not only possible to spend more and make the same ROI, sometimes you can saturate a given marketing channel and INCREASE your ROI from 3:1 to 4:1 or more.

What Should Be Tracked? Phone Calls? Emails? What Does 'Cost to Acquire a Customer' Mean?

Let's define a "qualified prospect" or potential client as a phone call, email, text or contact us form fill from someone who has a legal issue in your practice area(s) and metro.

Out of all the ways a lead can come in, a direct phone call is by far the strongest and best lead.

Even though potentials sometimes do fill in the contact us form on your website, send an email, use Live Chat, or text you, leads come in more rarely these ways, and are typically not as likely to become clients. Regardless, you must track any and all types of leads that you get.

Tracking teaches you a very important concept: what your **"Cost to Acquire a Customer"** is…

Let's say you spend $1 for each person that clicks an ad to get to your website. Tracking shows you that 1 of every 200 clickers pick up the phone and call you. (By the way, these are not unrealistic numbers - conversion online is very low)

This means you spent $200 to *just get a lead to call you*, never mind RETAIN YOU! ($1/click * 200 clicks/call)

It gets even more expensive and scarier…

Of the potential clients that call, what percent end up paying your retainer and hiring you? (your 'call to conversion ratio')

If you retain 1 in 3 callers, that means:
($200/call * 3 calls/retention) = **$600** to get a warm body in your chair, signing a retainer.

Now consider what you charge on a run of the mill, no trial, simple case. If you charge $1,000 and it costs you $600 to acquire a customer, that's not much of a profit margin. With court time and overhead, **you may lose money working on a case like this!**

What if a basic case is worth $2,500 to you on average (because you treat everyone like gold and don't offer the lowest price) and you're spending only $600?

Well, now you have 450% ROI, and you're making good money from your advertising.

This is why tracking and knowing your cost to acquire a customer, from each type of marketing you do, is CRITICAL.

It's worthwhile to figure out how much it costs you to get a client from each marketing channel. Chances are, you'll be shocked at how much marketing you have to do to get someone to sign your retainer agreement.

For most attorneys, cost to acquire a client is $500 to $1,000 – and sometimes a lot more.

Moral of the Story: If your prices are way low, you may be starving to death and not know exactly why. Know your cost to retain a client, get a phone call, email, text or contact us form filled in.

Remember: each lead you get costs a LOT of money, is precious, and must not be wasted with bad follow up.

Do You Use A Marketing / Advertising Sales Funnel? "If You Don't Know What A Funnel Is... Oh, Boy..."

A sales funnel is the series of steps, which a stranger takes on the path to becoming your retained client . These steps range from encountering your marketing, or advertising, all the way through signing your retainer agreement, through 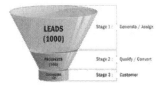 representation, through to past client status and beyond.

Once a potential client calls, emails, texts, or fills in a web form, a typical attorney will have a two or three-step sales funnel before actual retention occurs. We'll focus on this part.

Let's say potential client calls and you talk to them. They either book an appointment for an initial consult or say, "I'm going to ask around and call you back." That is the 1st step of this initial part of your sales funnel.

<u>A lot of attorneys lose people at Stage 1</u> for various reasons like mishandling calls and interactions, but also in large part because they never follow up. They lose 80%+ of the people who call because the prospect is unqualified; they're just a tire kicker or freeloader, or the attorney has bungled the

interaction by not inspiring trust, building a rapport, which led the person to price shop or get a second opinion.

Yes, I know that there are many price shoppers, tire kickers, and mentally ill people who have no intention of retaining EVER.

I can only help you with the ones who have some merit, so let's focus on those…

Moving along your sales funnel, we get to **appointment setting stage**. Some firms have tons of no-shows while some convert most callers on the phone, without even necessitating an in-office appointment!

If you have lots of no-shows or even a consistent percentage of no-shows, one big reason is that you're not following up with potential clients and thus reducing their "buyer's remorse" before their appointment time, which may be 2, 3 or 5 days in the future.

(We'll go much deeper into follow-up in the attorney-author-authority-process "speak a book" section of this book)

Remember, your appointments are being lured away by the siren songs of other attorneys, and the negative comments from friends, family, and a spouse or parent.

As a potential client moves further along your funnel, your client acquisition cost or the money you've spent to get those increases, and so each stage becomes more important to manage and patch holes.

Visualize the potential going down this funnel, getting closer and closer to the end point where they are signing your retainer agreement and putting money in your pocket.

Moving along the sales funnel to **Step 3** where the potential client successfully makes it in for an appointment. They're in your office now and you have spent $500 - $1,000 or more, plus a lot of time and effort just to get them in the door.

Are you going to convert them to a retained client, or are they going to say, "Well, I've got to talk to my wife. I'll be back."

Will you hear: "You're too expensive," or "I don't have the money."

Yes, we certainly will talk about strategies to help you minimize all these problems, but realize that this is another step in your funnel, and a lot is at stake at this point!

Diagnose Your Sales Funnel – Where's The Biggest Leak?

When you look at your sales funnel, you'll see that you're losing most of your clients at a certain step, versus the others. You want to fix this hole in your hose because this is from where the most water (MONEY) is leaking out.

Only by knowing <u>what your funnel is</u> and tracking and examining each step will you know the exact point at which you are losing people. You will surprise yourself once you've identified the problem and think, "Damn. We're losing thousands of dollars in retainers here… and I didn't even realize!"

Even at this point, I've heard the following from countless attorneys, still convinced that lead tracking isn't necessary:

"Well, I <u>Should</u> Track All My Marketing, But My Sales Funnel Isn't The Problem…Once I get someone in the office, they hire me 80% of the time."

…but what about all the potentials who no show appointments or give excuses on the initial free phone consultation?

Ever mystery shopped your own practice?

You'd probably cringe and want to crawl inside your own skin and hide if you did.

Using a disclaimer, you want to record every incoming call and every person who answers the phone, including **yourself**, your admins and any attorneys on staff.

I've heard many law firms (who claim to run a tight ship) screwing up potential client interactions and LOSING

CUSTOMERS even more frequently that firms who aren't so sure of their abilities.

Over 90% of the law firms I've mystery shopped (which has been hundreds) cause themselves to lose 20-60% of the clients they would otherwise get, due to poor handling of inbound calls and emails.

From secretaries that blurt out, "*Law Office!*" to attorneys that immediately interrogate potential clients, firms mishandle callers and make potential clients nervous way more often than you could imagine.

They fail to build rapport, fail to show genuine empathy for a nervous potential client's legal situation, and fail to treat potential clients as human beings.

They drive potential clients away.

How would you like to hear that callers to your law firm are put on hold for 5 minutes on average before being connected to you and that a third of them hang up?

Reality check: Nearly 50% of firms we've mystery shopped tell us: "The attorney's not in. Do you want his voice mail?" or "The attorney's not in. Please call back later."

A recent article on Car Dealerships said that **20% of all calls go unanswered.** Think about the next time someone cries that we're in a bad economy!

I've heard countless secretaries / admins talk rudely to people who, due to lack of an empathy, hang up on them.

Many attorneys are rude, abrasive, and scary to potential clients.

Are you a jerk? Are you a terse, unhelpful, "I can't tell you anything until you come into my office" attorney?

You'd be shocked (or perhaps not) at how many law firms are rude to potential callers.

This lack of attention can cost you dozens of lost clients, and $50,000 a year or more... EASILY.

I know you don't want to do it, but this is a hugely ignored area of marketing / advertising that is rarely tracked, tested, and tweaked.

Who wants to step on the scale when you're 400 pounds?

Who wants to hear from the doctor that they've got diabetes and high blood pressure?

No one – that's why you must track NOW so you don't mysteriously die of a financial disease later and never be the wiser.

Make sure you look at all your personnel NOW. Each one represents their own ROI - ask are they contributing to or financially draining your firm?

Analyzing all your personnel and their individual ROI / performance will help you diagnose the hidden virus in your office that's sabotaging new clients hiring you.

Let's say you have two attorneys working for you and two admins. You want to track the actual number of potential clients each one is interacting with vs. the number of clients retained - you may find one that has a much lower (or higher) conversion rate.

Regardless of WHY, you at least can "re-educate" or fire that person and adopt the methods of your top performer.
(Give the top performer a raise, too – incentivize all staff including yourself)

What Are The Easiest, Cheapest & Most Effective Tracking Methods Around?

Thankfully, it's easy and cheap to track nowadays. For phone tracking, you can use services like DialogTech.com, which I highly recommend.

Dialog Tech costs approximately $80 per month and includes one or more local or 1-800 tracking numbers. It's a cost effective way to have each call to and from your firm recorded, forwarded, and tracked.

Put unique phone numbers that forward to your main phone number on every marketing channel you use, and services like Dialog Tech can track them – it's simple, effective and eye-opening.

Where should you put tracking phone numbers?
On billboards, your business card, your website, everywhere!

For my clients, I put tracking numbers on their website, Google Maps listings, direct mail letters, billboards, Yellow Pages ads, Google Adwords, business cards, and as many places as makes sense .

A common frustration I hear is, "We have clients call us, but we don't know where they come from.

Then, when asked how they were referred to us, people say the internet or they don't know."

Well this way, you will know.
You don't have to depend on callers' poor memory.

Tracking can tell you a given person called the number on your billboard next to highway I-70, because that's the only place you used that unique phone number; it can tell you someone called from your website, or from your monthly e-newsletter.

You can tell when someone calls from your website, not just "the internet" or "Google".

Phone tracking is a VERY powerful tool.

What makes it even better is the data it gives you, such as: The date and time someone calls, their caller ID, the number of minutes they were connected, what marketing channel they came in on, and if you wish, literally what was said if you're using the call recording feature.

This is a real fast way to get the pulse on a new marketing idea or evaluate an existing marketing method. You'll quickly know if that newspaper ad, pay per click campaign, or online lead service is bringing in calls.

Also, tracking web form submissions and emails is very easy to set up on your website. If someone fills in and submits a form, it's a no-brainer to track and can be set up in minutes.

Once Tracking Is Set Up, Use SmartSheet.com's Online Shared Excel Sheets to See All Your Leads in Real Time

Getting tracking data is great, but if it's a pain to assemble, if it can't be updated in real time.

If multiple people in your firm need to update the results on the fly, then you need SmartSheet.com

(**Disclaimer:** SmartSheet and Dialog Tech do not compensate me for recommending them – I love both services, however)

Everyone in your firm must be committed to putting all the results for a given day in a common place like Smart Sheet in order for the data to be useful.

You can have it set up so that every phone call and every email coming in goes into one sheet that everyone can share and access at all times. When the call comes in, Jane upfront can update that it was a solicitor. When another call comes in, Joe the attorney can say, "Oh, I talked to them and we have an appointment for next Tuesday."

In a month's time, you'll have a simple report that says, "This month we received 34 phone calls and five web forms. Of all leads, nine were potential clients and we retained six. Their names were X, Y, and Z, and four of them came from our website, while one came from direct mail and another from a newsletter."

"Attorney Mike retained three of them. Jane, the admin, was involved in four of the six retainers. It cost us $642 per client for the four website retentions, $783 for the direct mail client and $376 for the newsletter client. Total gross revenue from all six clients was $17,400."

Can you see the power of knowing all of this through a simple method of tracking and finding out exactly what is happening in your firm?

Look at the difference between knowing this level of detailed conversion data versus hoping, guessing, and praying!

Final note: In order for this to work you have to make it **mandatory** that all your personnel, including you as the attorney, update this shared spreadsheet at least 3x a day; or whenever a client calls, emails or comes in.

Get tracking and grow your practice. For $100 a month or less in cost, it's a no-brainer.

HOLLYWOOD USES SCRIPTS...
...AND SO MUST YOU AND ALL STAFF

Everyone in your firm that interacts with the potential, current, and past clients should use scripts. I'm not talking about your admins / secretaries / answering service, or other attorneys in the firm. I am talking about **YOU**, too...

Why? There are three very important reasons.

#1 - You want to give the potential, current and past clients a consistently positive and fantastic experience when they call your law firm. (Yes, it IS possible to have a good experience calling a law firm) In the "Treating Clients Like Gold" section, you can read about the myriad reasons on why a great experience is vital to a successful practice.

#2 – Are you being sabotaged by rude, apathetic admins or secretaries, answering services or other attorneys in your firm? You may be sabotaging yourself by answering the phone rudely, not building rapport, and NOT scripting your calls. (Many attorneys are in for a nasty surprise when their practice is mystery shopped, only to find that THEY are the biggest problem)

#3 - Wouldn't you love to cut out the daily, relentless phone calls from solicitors who drain you and your staff's time?

There are a lot of time wasters out there – solicitors, court personnel, tire kickers and people with no money. A lot of attorneys blow a minimum of 1 – 2 hours a day on the phone with these knuckleheads.

Think about it. How many times a day does your office phone or cell phone ring? If you're answering most or all of the calls, then <u>you are getting way too many annoying and useless calls</u> from marketing companies, tire kickers, and time wasters, while <u>too few from potential clients</u>.

You must use your time wisely.

What if you have your personnel trained to screen calls effectively, only letting qualified prospect calls through?

What if you only talk to <u>real potential clients</u>?

I bet you would save at least an hour a day, and to an attorney, that's huge. Sharpen your gatekeepers' teeth. Train them to stick and move like Muhammad Ali and filter, screen, and block bad calls, while letting all the good ones through.

Here's a powerful sample script that filters like a charm:

Instead of answering the phone with, "Law office", your admins should instead say "Law Office of XYZ. This is Mary. Are you calling with a legal problem we can help you with?"

Why say this?

Right off the bat, the caller must identify themselves as a potential client, or a waste of time, or simply an annoying pest. If a caller does NOT have a legal problem, this question will filter the useless calls out.

Let's say the caller gets sneaky and says, "I'd like to speak to Attorney XYZ." What should your gatekeeper say in this instance?

"Attorney XYZ devotes his time to working on current client issues and talking to new potential clients who want his <u>undivided attention</u> and help. Do you need legal help, or are you a current client?"

Train the admins to sit and wait for the answer. The caller will then respond and say if they are a current client or that they truly want legal help.

Or alternatively, a caller may then say, "Well, I'm calling to speak to him about a marketing plan," or "I'm just trying to find out how much he charges."

If they don't need legal help and they're not a current client, then the gatekeeper should say, "Please give me a brief description of what you are going to tell Attorney XYZ before I see if he's available. I do not want to upset him by interrupting his important client work without good reason."

Once again, you're forcing people to qualify and filter themselves. NO, you're not being mean. A caller must have a deserving reason to get through to the busy attorney who wants to focus on his/her clients. What's mean about that?

See how this script acts as a powerful filter?

Most folks who aren't potential clients won't get through to waste <u>your time and your day</u>. Court personnel can be handled by the admin. Marketers can be screened out and forced to send an email or blocked completely.

Furthermore, you can CHOOSE to take certain calls from certain types of people when it's convenient for YOU. No more fighting fires all day. For instance, if you are truly in need of new marketing, you can block off a two-hour chunk on a Thursday morning to handle marketing calls.

- This script will save you at least an hour+ a day.

- It will improve your ability to retain new clients and improve your relationship with existing clients.

- Current clients will know that you are focused on their cases and that you take their situations very seriously because your admin said so!

- Potential clients will know that you focus heavily on your current clients and are assured of the same dedication once they retain you.

- Solicitors, court personnel, and other potential time-wasters will filter themselves out. They'll feel bad for disturbing you because you appealed to their better nature, saying, "This guy is working on important stuff. If you're not calling about that, I don't want to bother him."

Although scripts can be lifesavers and game changers, I also guarantee most attorneys reading this will find an excuse NOT to do it.

Here are the most common Assumptions / Excuses:
"Oh, my secretary won't do this. She's been with me for six long years. I can't tell her to do this now."

"We don't have a problem with how we answer the phone. We're fine. Answering the phone, "Law office" works just fine for us."

"I really don't get that many calls. This is not necessary and isn't going to help."

"I don't want to push away potential clients, and screening them would push them away."

"Clients know that I'm a lawyer. I'm busy and they shouldn't waste my time anyway, so I don't need this."

I've heard these excuses and assumptions a million times.

Don't fear scripting – welcome it. Why get in your own way and stop yourself from succeeding, like stepping on the gas pedal while the car is still in park?

Shave five hours a week off your work schedule.

Spend more time with your spouse and kids.

Allow yourself time to think, plan, and run a business.

Stop fighting fires all day and put scripting to work for you.

How Answering Your Phones The Wrong Way WILL (not may) Cost You Thousands In Lost Revenue

Now that you're convinced you should script your calls, I'm going to give examples of bad vs. good scripting.

When a potential calls your law office and you blurt out, "LAW OFFICE" it makes callers immediately uncomfortable and many will stutter and get nervous.

Bad way to start.

You didn't say which law office they called. You didn't greet them. You didn't say your name.

Seeking some sign of human life, a caller may uncomfortably say: "Is…thi…this…uh… the law office of John Smith?" Identify yourself with a <u>warmer greeting</u> such as, "Law office of Jones, Jones and Smith. This is Sarah. Do you have a legal issue that we can help you with?"

With this script, now they know **where they called**, <u>who they're talking to</u>, and a question has been put to them that they must answer.

Sounds obvious, right? Common sense is not very common.

Let's continue with the bad script. Someone says, "Law office" and the caller stammers, "Hi, I uh, got arrested last night for drunk driving. Are you an attorney? Can you help me?"

The admin says, "No, Mr. Smith is the attorney. He's on the phone right now. Can I take a message?"

The caller says, "Never mind, I'll call back. Bye."

This EXACT SCENARIO is so common, it's scary.

Well, now you have lost a potential. Why? You made them uncomfortable. With the reply, they didn't know if you were an attorney or an admin when they called. They had to tell you their problem, and for the caller, it is like calling out in the darkness, "Is anybody there?" If the caller DOESN'T hang up, you're still off on a very bad foot.

Most law offices are very unfriendly. It's <u>intimidating</u> to call an attorney and face your legal problem, especially when most folks rarely, if ever, run afoul of legal problems.

You hopefully have no idea of what it's like to face criminal charges. Or be a defendant in a civil suit. Or be facing divorce after 17 years of marriage. Or have a deportation order over your head. Or have to settle your uncle's estate.

Sure, you've spoken to many people in one or more of these situations as an attorney, but being a client yourself is a **completely different experience.**

People are emotional, upset, frightened, and freaked out.

If facing DUI or other criminal charges, they've been questioned by police, handcuffed, arrested, embarrassed, and might have sat in jail overnight or longer.

If they're facing divorce, their whole world might be melting down. If they're facing bankruptcy, they're feeling the sting and shame of screwing up financially. On and on it goes.

If a potential client is calling you, and you or your admins are rude, it is inevitable that they're going to hang up or at least question you, your motives, your experience, your fees, everything.

Here's another bad script:
(C = caller; S = secretary; A = attorney)

C: "Hi, uh do you guys know if a second shoplifting charge in six years counts as a first-time offense?"

S: "You'll have to ask Attorney Smith. Let me transfer you to him."

Wait a minute…
You didn't answer the person's question.

Meanwhile, in addition, some firms put callers on hold for 5+ minutes, and naturally the caller hangs up. By just transferring the caller and not telling them your name or asking simple screening questions, you've already dropped the ball.

The secretary <u>could have said</u>:

S: "Mr. Smith has worked with many clients who have similar situations. He'll be able to give you the details you need to handle this. I'm very sorry this happened to you. Please hold for a minute. I'm going to transfer you right away."

How much better does that sound versus, "Duh, I don't know anything? Let me transfer you."

When the call is transferred, how do you, as the attorney, answer?

A: "This is Attorney Smith," is NOT a good greeting.

There's no intro from your admin - it's not a warm transfer. The caller has to start again with their question, "Hi. Does it count if you have two shoplifting charges in six years as a first offense?"

Making the caller repeat their question further intimidates them. They're already starting to become annoyed, irritated and obviously stressed out. They're now on guard and suspicious.

Furthermore, they <u>haven't been given an indication or even a hint</u> that your law office "fights for you," "is aggressive," "has 27 years' experience," "is board-certified," or any of the jargon that lawyers' use in their marketing (jargon that clients do not understand or value).

You haven't done a single thing to show benefit or differentiate yourself before you started to interact with a potential client. *This is a lost opportunity*.

Here's a much better way to handle the call:

S: "Mr. Smith has worked with many clients who have similar situations. He'll be able to give you the details you need to handle this. I'm very sorry this happened to you. Please hold for a minute. I'm going to transfer you right away." (Same as before)

THEN, she calls the attorney and says "Hi, Attorney Smith. This is Sarah up front. I've got Bob on the phone. He's dealing with a second shoplifting charge in six years. He had a question for you as to whether that counts as a first offense or second. Can I put him through?"

Sarah then returns to the caller and gets the attorney on the line with the caller:

S: "Bob, this is Attorney Smith. He will definitely be able to help you with your shoplifting question."

A: "Hi Bob. I appreciate you calling... Sarah, we will take it from here – thank you."

Sarah says, in closing, "Thanks for calling Bob. I'll let you two talk things over. I'm hanging up now."

How much professionally better is that script versus a cold transfer with no hand-off? Wow.

Can you see why scripting can radically improve your retention rates and earn you more money without additional marketing?

Let's talk about what happens vs. what you should do during an initial phone consult with a potential client.

You're on the phone with a potential, and they've described their situation briefly. Typical attorneys would say, "Well, the law says this and that, and the maximum penalties are X, Y, and Z. You must come in for an appointment, and then we can go into your situation in depth. I can't say much or promise anything on the phone. You have to come in."

Instead of spending quality time on the phone of 15 or 30 minutes talking to a prospect and building rapport, most attorneys want to get them in the office to close. They're afraid to spend time on the phone for fear of wasting time and/or losing the potential client.

Sadly, the truth is just 'trying to get 'em in the office' often backfires and lowers your retention percentage. Why?

Even though your answers, using the above script are factual, they're **unemotional.**

- You're not addressing the true need of the person calling.
- You're not providing information.
- You're not building trust and rapport.
- **You're not giving any reason why and how you are <u>different</u> from any other attorney that they might talk to.**

How is a prospect supposed to figure out if they should come see you versus calling other attorneys if you haven't achieved any of the above bullet points?

Do you want to know what most callers will say or think, based on just 'trying to get them in the office'?

"It's okay, thanks. 'Click.' or "I have to talk to my wife, and then call you back. Bye."

Once they hang up, <u>they are NEVER going to call you back</u> and **<u>you know it</u>**.

Off they go, looking for another attorney that's not rude, or offers zero information, and/or tries to just "get them into the office."

Hopefully, this doesn't sound too familiar, if you're even <u>lucky enough to get this far,</u> because your admin, secretary, or answering service didn't screw it up even before the call got to you!

What's a better way to handle calls from potential clients?

Some superstar lawyers I have as clients retain nearly 70% of the potential clients that call them. They spend 30 minutes on the phone with each potential client.  They explain every step of the case process, give the likely sequence of events, explain the law and possible defenses, all the while concurrently evaluating and qualifying the potential client to see if it's worthwhile investing time in representing them.

By the end of a properly executed call, guess what happens?

➔ These attorneys often **<u>get hired and take payment right then and there, on the phone</u>**

They don't need the caller to come to the office. They have much fewer no-shows, delays, or chance for other attorneys to swoop in and seduce the potential clients away.

This is because **they did the work of building rapport, educating, trust-building and screening on the phone.**

Instead of believing that you're WASTING TIME during a phone call with a potential client, there is no better time spent building rapport, hearing their fact pattern, educating them, demonstrating you're a human being, a lawyer who cares, is personable, and has skills that will be of use to them.

If you don't do this, how will a prospect know that you're different, special, board-certified, caring, aggressive, or the right attorney for them?

They WON'T.

Remember, Hollywood uses scripts, and so must you.

Get the Credibility, Authority & Celebrity You Need to Dominate Your Competitors – How to Write and Publish A Consumer's Guide Book in Your Practice Area In Less Than 30 Days

Writing a book is not NEARLY as hard or time-sucking as you think, so don't get worried.

Authoring a book by 'speaking it', is a unique method I developed called the **Speak-a-Book**™ Process.

First of all, why go through the trouble?

Let's say your doctor tells you that you're barely three months away from a deadly heart attack and you must see a heart surgeon right away.

Can you simply call your favorite heart surgeon on their cell phone and book an appointment that's convenient for you?

The top specialists are booked for months, and I**f you are lucky**, you'll get an appointment two weeks out, on a day and time not of your choosing, but probably the last open slot available with the doctor.

When this doctor sees you, you're going to tell him, "Thank you so much for seeing me Doc."

You're THANKING someone who you're going to pay $100,000 to cut you open and operate on your heart?

You don't question that it's going to be hard to even get an appointment with the heart surgeon. A no, you're not going to get their cell phone number. Don't even bother asking.

Once the heart specialist looks you over, conducts the diagnosis and prescribes a treatment regimen (which may include life-threatening, but necessary surgery) are you going to argue? Nope.

Whatever he tells you to do, <u>you will listen</u>… Why?

The heart surgeon symbolizes AUTHORITY. CREDIBILITY. CELEBRITY. EXCLUSIVITY.

Be Perceived As Exclusive, More Credible, and Authoritative Than Competing Attorneys

Although it won't magically transform you into the #1 lawyer in Personal Injury (for example) in your metro, authoring a book will improve your positioning with potential clients, big time… if it's done properly.

Let's talk in terms you'll intimately know:

Who would you hire to defend your DUI, fight for custody of your kids in a nasty divorce, defend your drug possession case, handle your $3 million dollar estate, ensure you get disability payments, fight to settle your workman's comp claim or to get you compensation for a car accident?

Choices A, B, C, D, etc. are your typical attorneys who say, "I'm aggressive. I'll fight for you. I have 30 years of experience. I'm board certified. I'm a former prosecutor."

The Authority Choice is the attorney who can not only say the above but also say: "Please take this copy of my book on this particular subject called '10 Ways to Defend Your XYZ Case.' Even if we're not a fit to work together, you'll get a lot of useful information from reading it."

The majority of potential clients will definitely be swayed, impressed, and more likely to hire the guy or gal who authored the book.

In my mind, the attorney author instantly grows 4 inches taller, looks more handsome, seems nicer, and becomes more authoritative, knowledgeable, and "expert-like". He or she becomes the Suze Orman of family law, the Doctor Phil of estate planning, the F. Lee Bailey or Johnny Cochran of criminal defense.

Who would YOU rather hire?

<u>Amazing stats to consider:</u>

➔ Attorney authors have up to a 1/3 LOWER no-show rate when their book is sent overnight through Fed Ex to a potential client prior to their scheduled appointment, in a package that includes testimonials, a personal letter, and yes, the attorney's book.

➔ Reduces excuses which the clients give you when they don't hire you: "I'll be back", "Let me talk to my wife," "Let me get back to you", "You're too expensive," or "I don't have any money."

If you've been procrastinating writing a book for several years because you hate writing or just don't have the time, **I can interview a spoken book out of you in 90 minutes flat.**

The entire process takes 90 minutes of phone interview time and approximately 2 more hours for final corrections. Who can complain about 3 ½ hours of total time to write and publish a book for potential clients?

You'll retain several dozen additional clients you otherwise would've lost to competitors for years of using your book (unless the law changes dramatically in your practice area or state, perhaps even longer, which usually happens only after years' of time).

If your clients are worth $2,500 each to you, that's:
$2,500/client * 1/month * 12mo/yr = **$60,000 a YEAR.**
Ultimately, it's EASY to write one, two three or more books,
each on a separate area of your practice or sub-area.
(ex: 1st time DUI, Car Accidents, Surviving Divorce, etc)

Don't be afraid. Be EXCITED about what it will do for your
business, your Credibility, your Authority and your Celebrity
status as an attorney.

You will dramatically increase your income, retention ratio
and the quality of clients you get; a **no-brainer.**

***Short commercial note:** For more
information on the Speak a Book™ Process
and how to get a book done in the next 30
days, contact Jacobs & Whitehall:

(888) 570-7338
rj@speakeasymarketinginc.com
www.JacobsAndWhitehall.com

A Brief History of the Speak-a-Book™ Process

For three years, I provided 34,982 DUI leads to attorneys nationwide through group legal advertising on myDUIattorney.org.

I quickly grew to like and respect the hard working and ethically-driven guys and gals out there who represent their clients to the fullest and beyond.

My first strategy to improve an attorney's Celebrity, Authority, and Credibility status in the surrounding areas that they serve was to conduct a free video interview through Skype®  to be posted on YouTube, which also linked to their website.

Attorney's feedback to this strategy included: "Potentials saw my video on the web and they really liked it."

These potential clients ended up hiring them and mentioned 'liking their videos' as a deciding factor. Fantastic – a step forward already!

These videos were helping the attorneys get clients, and the ones I interviewed would beat out the other local guys because the interviews provided a personal exposure to the attorney that the potentials were seeking.

Upon seeing what the attorney looks like and hearing how they sound, the potential clients could develop an understanding of how that particular lawyer thinks, acts, and would interact with them if hired; all from the safety of the internet.

Comments from potential clients to these attorneys were: "I felt I got to know you before I even met you" and "Your videos made me feel comfortable."

These videos led to lawyers being hired more often. These video interviews, surprisingly, even started to show up on the blessed 1st page of Google - the Holy Grail for most attorneys, gaining them more exposure, and in turn, more clients.

After conducting about 30 of these interviews and talking to dozens of more lawyers, I learned the ins, outs, and the industry insider reality of being an attorney; overworked, underpaid, the whole world on a payment plan, clients that stop paying, and misguided judges not letting you withdraw.

I learned about 80-hour work weeks, battling lowball, newbie attorney competition, price-shopping potentials, no-shows, and deal-killing secretaries.

In my travels, mainly to marketing seminars, I began to run into super lawyers. I don't mean the magazine "Super Lawyers," but super successful lawyers who all attributed their success to good marketing.

One DUI and reckless speeding attorney I met makes $500,000+ a year and gets well over 20 phone leads a day – he handed me his iPhone and let me scroll down through the leads that day in his email. He wasn't lying.

Another savant in California in estate planning shared with me a 96% closing rate of potential clients who came to his office for a consult – <u>simply amazing</u>.

A car accident personal injury attorney in Canada sends a newsletter to his past clients, which helps earn him **<u>77% of all his new client business from past client referrals</u>**.

Amazing attorneys, doing amazing things.

It didn't take more than a few conversations to perceive the commonality amongst these super successful lawyers. All of them said that providing useful information and education to potentials through a book they had authored was a major leg that their success stood on. Their authored books, they insisted, have established them as an Authority; not a cheapo, bleed 'em and plead 'em attorney. They have become minor celebrities in their niche and local area, and whooped their competition's collective behinds in the process.

Potential clients, they insisted, were **attracted** to the non-threatening, educational resources that these attorneys had put out. Potential clients started to call more often while the tire kicking and the price shopping died way down. Clients were proactively coming to them versus the attorneys having to hunt and kill on a daily basis.

Motivated by what I heard, I adopted their book-mongering process and developed the **Speak-a-Book™ Process.**

How does it work?

First, you and I schedule a 15-minute discovery call to see if the Speak-a-Book™ Process is right for you. You choose how many books you're going to "speak" and their specific topics (ex: DUI, juvenile law, car accidents, drug cases, sex crimes, divorce, estate planning, etc.).

No one is ever caught off guard by the questions because they're all crafted and disclosed beforehand. Even if I have no previous experience with a topic, I ask you the most common questions that potential clients are asking you on a daily basis, as well as the layman's "urban myth" type questions you're likely to be asked, based on my television and mass media "education."

The goal is to re-create you in print: Your style, mannerisms, knowledge, and experience. It's a facsimile of your best phone consultation and your most compelling statements, all of which will turn prospects into retained clients. It's an educative and non-threatening "best of you" guide book.

Next, we schedule a 90-minute, recorded, Q&A interview-style phone call. The whole call is then transcribed, and the ums, yeahs, uhs, and other false starts are edited during the transcription phase.

My team then creates a title and crafts a cover design, incorporates testimonials, lays out the interior, makes chapters with a table of contents, adds relevant pictures and contact information, and sets up the whole book. It includes a disclaimer that the book is purely informational and is not to be taken as legal advice. Creation of an attorney-client relationship is also disclaimed.

Finally, you review the final cleaned-up product and make the final edits. **Within three weeks you have a ready-to-print, ready-to-publish BOOK that you've authored.**

Now discover all the places your book can go; where it can be used, re-used, re-purposed, and made to help you:

Place #1 - The book becomes a downloadable PDF-format e-book. We modify your website's design and enable an online view of the picture of the book cover, called an e-cover, for website visitors. It looks like a real book on the web, and a download button for a free download is provided.

When a potential client clicks to download your free book, they're asked to enter their name, phone number, and email address. The PDF

then downloads to their computer, and their information is recorded and emailed to you. They've now "raised their hand" and become a lead you can follow up with via phone and/or email. By downloading your free book, they've expressed their interest in the topic and silently said, "Mr. Attorney, I've downloaded your book because I'm interested in the subject and have a related legal issue. Please contact me."

I highly encourage you to contact the lead later the same day or the next day. Ask if they liked your book, what prompted them to download it, and start building rapport.

Place #2 – A 90-minute call typically turns into approximately 7,000 transcribed words, which then gets chopped up into a series of 11-14 articles that are placed appropriately, subject-wise, on your website.

This dramatically adds to your website's content and makes you more likely to rank highly in Google, Yahoo, and Bing organic searches. Your website becomes a compelling resource for searchers. It helps your SEO and website presence progressively for years to come.

Some of my attorney clients have smartly invested 8-10 hours of their time to create multiple books, and thereby add 60,000 – 80,000 additional words (100+ articles) to their websites.

These same attorneys have witnessed their organic traffic quadruple or more, and their phones are ringing more.

Place #3 - The books are physically printed. Many attorneys cringe at this step as they do not know how to effectively use the physical version of their book.
But the #1, Most Critical, Most Useful Way to use your book is to print physical copies and mail / hand them out to potential clients (More on this shortly).

First of all, printing is NOT expensive. An initial order of 100 copies comes to you within 7 business days of the order. The cost is $350-400, including shipping ($3.50 - $4.00 a book).

You'll definitely feel a sense of pride and accomplishment the day you receive your box o' books, tear it open, and hold them in your hands.

Place #4 - Take pictures of yourself proudly holding and displaying your book. Why? Again, it establishes your Credibility, Authority, and Celebrity status. Guess where you put these pictures?

They go on your website, on a Yellow Pages ad, on your business card, billboard, bus stop, your office walls – everywhere and anywhere. Any method of marketing that you have can use this picture to amplify your credibility. Let's say you do direct mail. Instead of standing in front of a shelf of law books, include a picture of you standing there holding a book you wrote. Trust me, it makes a big difference.

The Most Effective and Important Way
To Utilize Your Physical Book?

As previously mentioned, for client acquisition you have what is called a "sales funnel." Potential clients contact you by phone or email and go through a series of steps and either become a retained client or not.

Here's how to use your book to plug the holes in your sales funnel that are costing you $10,000 a month, or possibly more:

Scenario #1: A potential calls you and you engage in a phone consult. It sounds like they have a solid fact pattern, and they would make a good, profitable client, but they don't book an appointment. Instead, after spending a good 15-30 minutes with you or your admin on the phone, they say, "I'm going to call some other attorneys and get back to you," or "I'm going to talk to my wife about it," or "Let me think about it."

Shoot... I've wasted my time and the client isn't coming back. What do I do?

Typically, this indicates the beginning of the client's transition from potential to ghost ... You call them a couple of times, send an email or two, but they disappear into thin air and never return your advances again. Now what should you do instead?

Train your admin and yourself so that anytime a potential client calls your office, you say after the first sentence or two, "Just in case we get cut off Mr. / Miss X, let me get your name, address, phone number, and email."

Capture every potential's information so that you CAN follow up and get back to them.

If the caller is viable at all as a client, that same day, you or your admin must Fed-Ex, OVERNIGHT, a package to the potential, which will include your book, a sheet of testimonials, and a personal letter from you. Yes, it will  cost $10-$20 per potential client. So freaking what? This is NOT expensive.

If you do this for 10 potential clients a month, it amounts to $150-$200 a month. Consider: When this earns you 1-2 or more extra clients, is it still expensive?

Why does this work so well? Normally, a potential client does call several attorneys to evaluate. Most attorneys will sound about the same. Maybe one attorney sounds better than the other, but hiring an attorney requires deep thought, reflection, and bank account checking; never mind trust and belief that they've found "the right one." So many hurdles to overcome. But…

The next day, they get your package in the mail.

The potential says, "Oh, I remember that guy! He wrote a book?" This immediately builds a recall value. "Wow. Impressive. Here are testimonials from people who've hired him and obviously believed in him. He's credible. People seem to really like this guy. He's even taken the time to write me a personal letter and Fed-Ex this package to me and spend money on me!"

Compare the emotional, logical, and influential impact that your package will have compared to other law firms that just call the person three or four times to harass them by phone. This distinguishes you from the pack and gives you tremendous Authority, Credibility, and Celebrity status.

<u>Scenario #2:</u> You do a phone consult with a potential, just like before. Everything is going well and they make an appointment with you 2+ days in the future. REPEAT the exact same thing as in Scenario #1. Overnight the book, testimonials, and a letter from you. Follow the same script: "Just in case we get cut off Mr. X, let me get your name, address, phone number and email."

<u>In addition, here's what else you or your admin should say</u>: "I look forward to meeting you next Friday. In preparation for our meeting, I am Fed-Ex'ing you some very useful and important information in the mail. You'll receive it in the next day or so, so be on the lookout! It may ease your mind about what will happen moving forward. It is a book that Attorney <your name> wrote in the area of law you're having problems with. <u>Even if we aren't a fit and can't work together, you'll be well-prepared to hire the right attorney for you.</u>"

Even though they've made an appointment with you, guess what's happening in the potential's world the moment they hang up that phone? They talk to friends and family about their upcoming appointment with you. Well-meaning friends and family cast major doubt on the potential client's decision. They remind the caller that Uncle Bobby is a lawyer and can do the job a lot cheaper. Meanwhile, other attorneys are calling, harassing, seducing, lowballing, emailing, and pitching your potential client.

There's a lot of noise and major "buyer's remorse" going on.

Your book, testimonials, and letter are going to cut through all the noise, fear, uncertainty, and doubt.

The Fed-Ex package will cast away the doubt. There is the fear of meeting you in person; the fear of dealing with the legal issues; the doubt cast by their friends and family over their decision; doubt in themselves that they aren't guilty and shouldn't give up. Then, *voila*! Just in time, they get your package in the mail and the dial on the chorus of doubts gets turned way, way down.

Your no-show becomes a 'For Sure'

<u>Scenario #3:</u> Your initial phone consult leads to the booking of an office appointment, and the potential actually shows up for their in-office appointment…you conduct the consultation… **but** they give an excuse for not retaining you right then and there… and now they're about to walk out the door – what do you do?

You've spent a lot of time, effort, investment - $500 to $800 in marketing money (on average) **in getting this potential to come to your office and hear your initial consultation!** *Don't Forget That.*

About to walk out the door, the potential may give excuses and tell you: "I'll be back," or "I need to speak to my wife," or "I have to think about it," or even worse, "You're too expensive," or "I don't have the money" or "I just can't afford it."

<u>Before they walk out that door</u>, hand them the book you wrote, a sheet of testimonials, and a letter from you, and tell them the following:

"I want you to have a resource that will help you with your decision. Here's a book I authored about X area of law. The reason I

wrote it is to fully answer any un-asked or lingering questions people have about {subject area}.

It may be extremely useful and informative for you, and funny enough, it often inspires people to think of more questions.

Even if you decide we're not a fit and can't work together, this will help you make a more informed decision."

Compare the effect of giving the prospect your book, testimonials, and letter versus:

"Bye, bye, see you later. I hope to hear from you soon."

You're reading this book this very moment. What effect is it having on YOU?

You now know about three of the areas of your sales funnel where you should use the physical book you authored and why.

Re-cap of the Benefits of a Physical Book and Credibility Package:

- Retain a MUCH higher percentage of clients.
- Increase your Authority, Credibility, and Celebrity status in the eyes of potential clients.
- Retain a higher QUALITY of client. Tire kickers and cheapskates will weed themselves out.

- Cut down on "no-shows, be-backs, call-you-later, talk-to-my-wife, gotta-think-about-it, I-don't-have-enough-money" excuses.
- Command higher fees for your work due to your elevated status vs. other attorney competitors.

Consider: How would you like to retain more clients by spending just a fraction of a normal marketing budget?

Tighten up your sales funnel, and you can get off the treadmill of chasing more and more marketing channels.

Now, Let's Talk About EXCUSES Why 99% of Attorneys Sadly WON'T Author a Book or Tighten Up Their Sales Funnel

I call the first few excuses 'Goldie Locks Syndrome':

#1 - "The book is too thin. No one is going to read it. It's too flimsy." A 90-minute Q&A interview-style recorded, transcribed call actually converts into a 50-60 page, 5 1/2" x 8-1/2" glossy cover paperback book.

#2 - "The book is too thick. No one will ever read it." Wait a minute! I thought the book was too thin and flimsy – now someone else is complaining it's too THICK?

#3 - "Nobody is going to read this. People don't read anymore. They just look at their smartphones and iPads."

(Psst!) Aren't you READING this book at this very moment? People read and invest time in what interests them.

Happy Fact: Merely the act of the potential clients holding the book in their hands and thumbing through it for five seconds accords you 90% of the benefit of authoring the book.

Maybe 1 in 100 people will read this entire book. However, a vast majority will at least thumb through it, become impressed, read the testimonials, and maybe read through the first few and last few pages. Some will scan the table of contents and might even read a particularly interesting or relevant chapter.

Let go of the 'Goldie Locks Syndrome'; too thick, too thin, too this, too that. This stuff WORKS.

...MORE Excuses

"The book should be written as a regular textbook-style book; not an interview. *It must be professional*."

People want relevant information presented interestingly, not via a textbook. They won't tolerate being bored to death. People want to be entertained, and a boring, "professional," and dry book filled with legalese is not going to interest anyone.

These books are in interview format because it's far more interesting to read dialogue based content than textbook material. Who wants to be preached to? People have questions that demand an answer in a way that they can easily understand. That's what the interview format does – **it recreates the back and forth interaction of an initial consult by phone or in person.**

What happens if your book addresses all the common questions the potential clients have relentlessly been asking you, over and over, for the past 5, 10, or 20 years? The book will inform, entertain, and instill a sense of gratitude, respect, and awe of your knowledge and abilities – **you'll become the obvious choice to hire, price be-damned.**

...Even MORE Excuses

"It costs too much to do a book." Did you know that most companies charge $20,000 - $40,000 to publish your book, never mind helping you CREATE IT?!

In the honest spirit of making this business marketing tool accessible to hard-working attorneys who aren't rolling in the dough (yet), it's currently way underpriced, ranging from $4,000 - $6,000, including 100 physical copies, shipped right to your doorstep.

At this price, even if you only retain ONE MORE CLIENT than you would have, the book already pays for itself.

Your book will last you at the very least two years, and/or until the laws in your practice area significantly change - and then you can always update it.

Excuse #5,837: "I don't have the time to author a book." If you don't have an hour to spend speaking your book and an hour or two to make final corrections, then you don't have time to read this book either – so just give up and pray for a miracle.

AVOIDING A HOSTAGE SITUATION WITH YOUR VENDORS

Forget about just being "burned", many an attorney have been taken hostage by their web person, SEO guy, or marketing firm, pay per click company, or Google® Maps Optimizer.

I'm not exaggerating, and
No, this isn't a ridiculous statement.

I've heard dozens of horror and hostage stories from attorneys.

Does this sound familiar to you?

A law firm hires a company to build them a website and the company says that it will take three months. An entire year passes, filled with excuses, delays, and utter lies, and the website that goes live on the internet is only 70% finished. You paid the web designer thousands only to end up with a piece of junk that's not even fully functional.

Here's a common hostage situation:
You sign a one or two-year contract with an SEO and website design company. You're promised a new website and SEO work for the contract term. You're told that you won't have to

blog and that all the content for your website will be written by the company's "in-house professional staff".

How will the project progress be tracked? By the company's "proprietary client dashboard."

Who will handle your account? An overly happy, sunshine up-your-behind-blowing, account rep who puts!! **exclamation marks!!!** at the end of each sentence in their emails and WRITES IN ALL CAPS.

Here's what you DON'T KNOW: Many of these companies put your website up on a domain name that *they own*, NOT YOU.

Let's say you practice criminal defense in Minneapolis, Minnesota and the company you've contracted sets up your website on MinnesotaCrimDefense.com. (<u>Disclaimer:</u> not a real website at the time of this publication)

<u>Scary Fact:</u> **90% of 400+ attorneys I've spoken to don't even know if they own their own domain name.**

I find this amazing, scary, tragic, and therefore, worth mentioning. Don't you?

Note: If you don't own your own domain name, you certainly don't own any of the articles, images (i.e. 'content'), web traffic, or anything else associated with the website; **YET YOU ARE PAYING FOR IT.**

Doesn't that seem to you like a future hostage situation, just begging to happen? Once your contract term is up with these website terrorists, it's time for the hostage situation. You've paid thousands of dollars to have them design, supposedly SEO your website, fill it with content, and now your contract is nearing its end.

Unless you agree to the design company terrorists' new terms and payment amounts, what recourse do you have? Stop paying and the lights are turned off. The sign on the door gets changed to the next sucker and you're left with absolutely nothing.

Oh, but don't worry – you can always "buy out" your contract to own your content and maybe even the domain name for just $12,000 - $15,000. No problem at all!

Any account that you do not own and control access to is a future liability, headache, nightmare, and hostage situation.

Own every single blessed account that you use in your business. Own your domain name, your hosting, your Google+, Google Places, Google Analytics, etc. Own your phone numbers own everything.

You will say: "How should I interact with my vendors?" Give them access to your accounts with a login and password. Then, at 2 in the morning when you're lying in bed, tossing and turning and having nightmares about not getting enough clients, you can grab your iPad or laptop, log in, change the passwords, and go back to sleep a happy lawyer.

The next day, if your vendor freaks out because they want to access the account for promotional activity, they can do nothing to hurt you. If your vendor says nothing for weeks or a month, then it's positive proof that the vendor isn't even doing anything for you; just draining you of your money.

The Mechanics of Domain Names & Hosting

The place where you buy your domain name is called your **"Domain Name Registrar"**. Buying a domain name for a year is dirt cheap, currently costing about $15. Instead of buying a domain name for 1 year and worrying about renewing it, I would spend $60 and buy a domain name for 3-5 years.

Once your business has a domain name, you have to **host it** somewhere. A hosting company takes the files that make up your website – and that's what your website "is" –just a bunch of computer files–and puts them onto their computer servers that are connected to the internet. Then they hook up the networking plumbing to ensure that your websites show up when someone puts in your domain name, or eventually, searches in Google, Yahoo or Bing and you show up in organic search results.

Usually, your domain name registrar will also host your website. If not, there are tons of hosting companies out there.

Hosting isn't expensive either and runs about $20 a month. You don't want to go with the cheapest hosting because it's not actually worth it in the end. Going with something middle of the road around $20 a month, is fine for almost every attorney that I've talked to. Some like hostgator.com and almost everyone knows Go Daddy, Liquid Web, and Rackspace. There are a lot of places you can get hosting.

What is Content?

Any articles, pictures, captions, videos or other consumable information featured on your website is called "content."

Your content is intellectual property and can have substantial value. Don't shortchange it.

Beware of content, which is being created for you by third party companies, article writers or video companies. Just like not owning your domain name or hosting or any other account, you must ensure to get signed releases from any content writers, videographers, or photographers. These releases should give you 100% unrestricted use of the content that they create for you.

It doesn't matter if you have paid for it – make sure to get the rights to it all and have it documented or you will be headed for trouble down the road.

Common Content Horror Story

Let's say you have a two-year contract with a certain company. Your contract stipulates that you're renting the content – the web company creates it on your behalf, yet they own it.

Near the contract's end, you decide that you want to change providers or stop using this company. The account rep of the company says, "You have to pay us $10,000 to buy and keep the rights to your content and the content itself, otherwise, we have no choice but to take it all down."

How would you like to wake up to a skeleton website? A useless, stripped domain? One entire year of trying to get ranked in Google and get web visitors will be gone because your content will be gone. Within about a week, all your visitors from Google, Yahoo, and Bing will go to zero because your website is now empty … and the worst part?

You're legally plagiarizing if you copy and keep that information on your website. You'll have to write all new content. Talk about getting screwed over!

Hostage situations like this come about because attorneys don't realize that their website becomes an asset over time and can be worth A LOT of MONEY.

Don't Overlook This: For all parts of your profile, presence and visibility on the web- such as Facebook, Twitter, LinkedIn, Google Adwords Pay Per Click, Google Maps, Google Local, Google Plus, Google Analytics, Yahoo, Bing, Yellow book, Yellow Pages, CitySearch, Judy's Book, Merchant Circle, Yelp, AVVO, FindLaw, etc, you must have the log in and password for every single account.

The same hostage situation can and will happen when the time comes if you don't have the passwords. Tie down all potential loose cannons NOW.

As an attorney, you know relationships often start out beautiful and rosy and then turn to hatred and bickering when parties start to disagree. Word to the wise: (and you attorneys SHOULD be wise) Own everything- all logins and passwords. This way you can lock out anyone you want at any time and control all that is said about you on the web.

Otherwise, you're headed for disaster
And *it's no one else's fault but your own.*

Why Your Website Can Be So Much More Than You Ever Thought Possible

Your website is your intellectual property. You spend thousands of dollars and often years to develop it. It is something that can stay with you for many years to come. It <u>is your asset</u> and you have to treat and value it as one.

You can also be held liable if your content is not bar-compliant or misleading. You really have to ensure you have a responsible web presence and take care of your website to guarantee you own and benefit from it in every sense of the word.

One of the most exciting benefits of owning and building a good website is it's far-reaching and impactful ability to attract and bring you potential clients.

<u>**Did you know**</u> that it's not uncommon for a properly cared for, curated, SEO'd, and content-rich attorney website to CONSISTENTLY ATTRACT 3, 5, even 8 potential clients a month, month in and month out?

How much can your website be worth to you?

Let's say you're a DUI / DWI attorney and you charge $2,500 for a low-end, 1ˢᵗ time DUI case with no trial needed. Your website is two years old, has been SEO'd and content-rich from day one, and is now getting 75 unique visitors from Google / Yahoo / Bing every day.

On average, you get 24 calls a month from potential clients and convert 15%, which is about 4 clients a month.

4 clients/month * $2,500/client = $10,000 a month gross retention revenue.

$10,000 / month * 12 months/yr = $120,000 a year gross revenue from your website alone.

Expenses? Your SEO company is a good one, and they charge a fair amount → $1,000 a month ($12k/yr).

Your website now nets you $120k - $12k = $108k a year

$108,000 a year from your website.
How do ya like dem' assets?

…and when you go to retire and either sell your practice, sell out to a partner or close your doors?

You now have an asset that is very reasonably valued at 1x yearly net earnings of $108,000.

"…and that's the triple truth, Ruth." – Samuel Jackson's character in the movie, 'Do the Right Thing'.

WHY RANKING AT THE TOP OF GOOGLE RARELY EARNS YOU MORE CLIENTS

I'm not saying this just to be contrarian or to shock you, but you have every right to know the truth: If you've been sold on the collective fantasy that getting to be #1 on Google for a few, juicy, select keywords is the key to internet riches, then you're on a wild goose chase with an unhappy end.

Getting to #1 in Google for a few keywords is a meaningless waste of time, and I'm going to explain 'why' to you, using my personal experience; not theory or fantasy.

Every attorney thinks that people <u>mostly search a few, coveted, particular phrases </u>in Google and it's just not true. Some of the dream attorney keywords I've heard are:

- New York City auto accident lawyer
- Dallas DWI attorney
- Probation violation attorney
- Orlando sex crime lawyers
- Los Angeles criminal defense

You may ask: **"So how do I know** that chasing these particular keywords and others like them is a waste of time?"

I grew myDUIattorney.org starting from ZERO unique Google searches. The website is a group attorney advertisement where people arrested for drunk driving nationwide can enter in their information that is directly passed on to a DUI / Criminal Defense attorney in or near their zip code.

> _As of February 2013, Google sends 1,100+ UNIQUE searchers a day (33,000+ visitors a month)._

MyDUIattorney.org has helped deliver over 35,000 DUI leads since mid-2010.

Would YOU call that successful?

Go ahead and Google the website using various fantasy keywords and you probably won't see it show up in Google search – so how the heck does it consistently get 33,000+ visits for many months now?

> **About 18 months ago the site used to be #1 in Google nationally for "DUI attorney" and "DUI lawyer".**

Can you guess how many Google searches came from being on top of the world for the juiciest two terms in the DUI world? Not hundreds, not thousands but about 8 searches a day for each of those two keywords. **Think about that.**

We got 33,000 searches a month and 16 of them were from the dream keywords every attorney fantasizes about.

Guess how many different keywords made up the 33,000 searches a month?

➜ 25,794 Different Keywords

Just think about what that means: In simple terms, if only a few keywords were important out of 33,000 searches, we would have seen maybe 500 different keywords. Instead, over 80% of all searches were UNIQUE and DIFFERENT.

And the searches were NOT the typical searches what you think they'd be – they were all kinds of crazy sentences people type in when they've been arrested for DUI, such as:

- Arrested in San Francisco and blew .11 now what?
- 2nd DUI will I go to jail?
- Cop said I failed breathalyzer but I wasn't drunk
- Best attorneys in Milwaukee who take payment plans on drunk driving cases

This makes it amply clear - you tell me, how important is it to be on the top of the first page of Google for any one particular keyword or a small set of keywords? It is a meaningless waste of time. I have proved this successfully.

Google, itself has said: "50% of all searches on any given day are UNIQUE" – i.e. they have NEVER BEEN TYPED IN BEFORE.

But what does Google know? **They only control 84%+ of all search engine traffic.** _They only made $46 BILLION in 2012_ from people googling endless billions of different keyword phrases.

So it is evident that not only are the precious, bejeweled, coveted keywords everyone fantasizes about not really bringing in very many searches from Google. No one, <u>not even the people searching themselves</u>, know what keywords you SHOULD be on Page 1 of Google for.

So how the devil do you successfully do SEO?

Probably no other topic drives me crazier! I hear attorney after attorney complaining about their competitor being above them in Google for one or two glorious keywords that they're lusting after. I hear this relentlessly every single day, and it's a wild goose chase – a waste of time.

Oh, and by the way, what makes it even worse is that you would be hard pressed to find ANY SEO COMPANY out there that <u>doesn't claim</u>, "We'll get you to the top of Google. We'll get you on page 1 for 10 keywords. We guarantee you'll get in Google Maps, or appear for this keyword."

Note: It's fake science, complete bull, a false messiah, a wasted journey. Ninety-nine percent of attorneys are misinformed about page one of Google, but not you dear reader. Not anymore.

Why Haven't You Heard About This Before?
Is There a Google Conspiracy?

You have to go pretty deep into the SEO concepts to understand how online search behavior truly works.

I've spent 3+ years attending marketing conferences, studying Google and the other search engines. I talked to experts in the field, and pursued my passion for SEO and marketing in general to learn this knowledge, which I'm sharing with you.

Ninety-nine percent of SEO companies aim to sell you the red or blue widget off the shelf, real results be-damned.

Selling page 1 of Google for 10 top keywords is sexy – <u>the truth is not</u>.

So are you still skeptical? Go ahead and call my live attorney references that are listed on SpeakEasyMarketingInc.com or call me and I'll give you the contact of 20 more attorneys to talk to. My attorney clients are tremendously diversified in terms of SEO and content categorizations. Some of my top clients get 100+ Google searches a DAY, which makes their phones ring every single day with potential clients.

All the while, other uninformed attorneys are starving to death and chasing the same worthless, phantom keywords.

Here's WHY 50% of all searches are new and why a few, lame keywords form a tiny minority of what people search:

When you *"google"* something, you're compressing your entire problem, your emotions, and your thoughts into a few words inside a  Google search box. Google searches and searchers are as unique, different and varied as there are people in the world.

Every day people search for information that no one is, nor CAN directly SEO for because the searchers themselves are making up their search queries on the fly. They are depending on Google to give them the answer they're looking for from a sentence fragment or laymen's method of compressing their desire into a few words.

<u>Another fact:</u> Over 95% of people typically never make it past the first page of Google during an online search; so yes it IS vital to be on the 1st page of Google for the "right" search terms…

…but for 10,000 keywords that are thematically related to what you offer; not word-for-word specific.

Think about the keywords for which you want to be on page 1 of Google. Imagine each of them as a dandelion, with the specific dream keyword as the small seeded center. The hundreds of related keywords to your specific keyword are the white, fluffy hairs and strands of the dandelion – they make up a diffuse cloud – a THEME that you want to show up in Google for.

How to Get On the 1st Page of Google for 10,000 Different Keywords:

The answer is only - content, content and more content – i.e. 'words' found in online articles. Google can't read images yet, nor can Google translate videos or read Flash programming language (fancy moving graphics on websites).

Google's search engine ranking algorithm reads and relies upon TEXT – words, phrases, sentences, and articles.

<u>Example #1:</u> Someone is searching to find information on 'the consequences of refusing a breath test in Boston, Massachusetts, on a 2nd DUI offense'. Chances are that you will show up for that search on page 1 of Google if you're a Boston, Massachusetts attorney, (it's also where you practice DUI defense specifically) and you've written **an article** specifically about breath test refusals and their consequences for 1st vs. multiple DUI offenses. You also have to have a strong website that has many relevant links from other good websites to yours. (More on that shortly)

<u>Example #2:</u> Someone is searching for help with a "shoplifting charge in Austin, Texas'. They had a prior four years ago and want to know the look back period and if they'll have mandatory jail time on the 2nd offense.

You want to make sure, as a specialized attorney who handles theft crimes, that you have an article specific to this scenario. Again that is a site with a good number of popular relevant links.

Consider: If you built up 200 different articles on your website covering every aspect of the law that you practice. You adequately cover all frequently asked questions, subject areas, penalties, defenses, and even minutiae of various situations.

You'll start to appear on page 1 of Google (and even at the top of many 1ˢᵗ pages of Google) for THOUSANDS of different keywords or more; NOT just 10 or 20.

You won't essentially know what those keywords are and neither will anyone else until people actually start searching and your website shows up in Google search.

If you install Google Analytics (a free program that shows you what people type in to find your website through their search engine) **you'll start to see what searchers are ACTUALLY typing in to find you** – and yes, you'll be very surprised.

With several relevant articles on your site and more added over time, you'll start getting a lot of Google searches every day. It's

Google Analytics

definitely possible to build up to 100+ organic searches a day for a local attorney after about 12-18 months' worth of SEO.

These many searches will get your phone ringing every single day with potential clients. Some of my attorney clients have been patient enough to let me progressively grow their websites to this level and beyond.

These attorneys are killing it in Google, and the most beautiful thing of all? These informed attorneys are succeeding below the radar because their websites aren't showing up at the top of Google for the worthless dream keywords everyone cries out for.

Just like with myDUIattorney.org and other successful websites, **out of 100 searches a day, 90+ will be _different._**

If you think that this phenomenon of the "Long Tail" occurs just with SEO, you'd be surprised to learn, it happens with Google Adwords (Pay Per Click), Google Maps, and in every single area of online advertising where people search for answers.

ONLY diverse content (lots of articles on every aspect of your practice areas) will get you a listing on page 1 of Google for thousands of keywords.

Several hundred articles on your website, each of which addresses specific concerns or a tight theme of concerns, are what you need to have a successful site.

Here's an example of the articles possible (and needed) in the **DUI defense world:**

- Common misconceptions of people about their arrest
- Unintentional mistakes people make during and after their arrest that negatively affects their case and their potential outcomes
- If you fail Field Sobriety Tests, are you doomed to be convicted?
- What happens if you refuse the breath or blood test once you've been arrested?
- What are the driver's license consequences of a DUI arrest and/or conviction?
- How do penalties, both criminal and administrative, escalate for 2nd, 3rd, or multiple offenders?
- Why hire a lawyer who focuses on DUI vs. a general criminal defense lawyer or public defender?

Here's an example of the articles possible (and needed) in the **Car accident world:**

- Am I obligated to provide a statement to the other party's insurance adjuster? They're calling me off the hook
- Why not immediately seeing a doctor and documenting your injuries may hurt your ability to collect
- Common misconceptions people have about car accidents and lawsuits to "get the money they deserve"
- If I am in a collision with an underinsured or uninsured motorist, does that mean I can't collect any compensation?

If I'm searching for information about my DUI arrest, my domestic violence charge, my auto accident, my possible bankruptcy, etc, and…

…**If I come to your site and immediately see you specifically addressed my problem or question regarding legal aid, I am calling <u>YOU;</u>** not the 500 other attorneys who have the same, boilerplate gobbledygook content on their sites, stuffed full of keywords.

Does the following sound familiar?

"A Los Angeles DUI is a serious offense. You want to hire an experienced, aggressive Los Angeles DUI attorney to fight your DUI charges in Los Angeles."

Oh, and by the way, did I mention Los Angeles DUI 10 times in the first paragraph? Now does this make for informative reading? No. Google's search engine knows it is a garbage filler as well.

Lastly, the content strategy I've laid out here is what works in Google today in 2013, and it is not going to change anytime soon. Google demands unique, informative, relevant content, so playing by their rules only benefits you.

So please, don't be a lemming. Be cautious and don't be lured onto the rocks by the siren song of 10 garbage keywords on page 1 of Google. Go for 10,000 keywords instead.

Giant Swiss Cheese or Huge Spider Web –How Visitors ACTUALLY Interact with your Website

Bad websites look like the movie set of an Old West town. Your website has a painted, landscaped, beautiful front façade / front yard / **Homepage**.

But as soon as you walk behind the front façade, you see that the back and sides are completely empty and they're held up by a wood frame of 2x4s.

Real, impactful websites look like 3-D spider webs or a gigantic wheel of Swiss cheese with lots of holes.

→ Visitors who search "the web" (pun intended) may be caught in the kill zone of your spider website from any strand, in any direction.

→ Information hungry mice (Google searchers) can enter in through hundreds of holes in your wheel of Swiss cheese.

Most folks think that all website visitors enter through their homepage. This is a serious misconception. This leads you and the website designer to spend way too much time on your homepage and neglect all the other pages of your website.

Do you know how Google works? Did you know that each page of your website will preferentially appear in Google for specific keywords? Suppose you have a page about Domestic Violence penalties, but your website also contains pages on Theft Crimes, DUI, Weapons Offenses, etc. If someone Googles, *"Will I have a mandatory jail for a 1ˢᵗ domestic violence charge?"* Google will show THAT particular page in its search results; NOT your homepage.

Makes sense, doesn't it? **Because your domestic violence page is the most relevant to that person's search, NOT your homepage, Google shows THAT page.**

Once you realize that every single page of your website can and will be landed on by people searching Google, you no longer have a website – you have a spider web or giant wheel of Swiss cheese – choose your favorite image.

You may ask: Why does this happen? Understand that if Google didn't do a damn good job matching people's search with the most relevant search results, Yahoo or Bing would be internet king.

Instead, Google controls 80% of all searches and makes over $46 billion a year from search marketing. Needless to say, Google knows what the heck it is doing.

Now **do you see how you can get to page 1 of Google for thousands of keyword searches?**

Each page of your website has a chance to appear on the 1st page of Google for the theme of keywords it has in it – the content that it contains.

Note: Your homepage can be beautifully optimized and compelling, but if the other pages look like garbage, you sure do have a big problem.

Every page of your website has to:

- Be compelling, informative, and straight to the point
- Immediately answer a searcher's question, without having to hunt around for the answer
- Look pleasing to the eye and easily navigable
- Pull visitors deeper into your site and engage them, not have them bounce (click the 'back button' to leave the site) without visiting another 2nd or 3rd page.

To make a profitable website, not only do you want to have many articles that discuss all the details of your practice areas, you have to ADD to your content consistently over time and grow it. Mice don't want a small, moldy piece of cheese and won't bite. Flies won't fly into a tiny web of breakable strands. Google won't favor a content-poor website.

Keep these pictures in mind. The sooner you can visualize your website for how it can get visitors using these two images, the better you can craft your strategy of attracting, trapping and retaining mice, flies or the potential clients.

How to Attract, Educate, Show Credibility & Authority To Compel Potentials to Call Your Office or Fill In Your 'Contact Us' Form

Here I share some specific strategies I use to get my attorney-client websites more visitors, make the visits "stickier", last longer, and compel more potentials to call and to eventually retain them as clients:

#1: Create and Offer a book (or guide) the website visitors can download for free that will educate them on a specific practice area or topic. Examples of such guides/books can be found on my attorney-client websites, with titles such as: "Milwaukee DUI Arrest? Useful Info Revealed That May Help Your Case".

Your free book / guide acts as bait when potentials visit your website. It shows them your authority and credibility. It offers them a non-threatening way to learn more without having to call you and hearing the usual sales pitch.

Provide the book link on every page. Whatever page they land on or navigate to, they can grab your free content, download, read it and then come back and call your office and potentially hire you.

#2: Write tons of content / articles on all kinds of specifics. Show your site visitors that you, as an attorney, know exactly what's bugging them and how you can help. Let's say a potential is searching whether they are going to jail for 2nd time DUI charges where they blew above a .15. If your website has an article that talks specifically about this, they're going to think, "Wow, this attorney has an answer that addresses **MY PARTICULAR SITUATION**. I am going to call him/her."

#3: Necessarily have related articles widget on every single article page. This will give people a logical way to further explore your site and go deeper to find the answers to their search. This helps pull people deeper into the site. Let's say a potential searches Google for: "failed field sobriety test."

You should have related articles that are titled:
- If you fail the field sobriety tests, are you automatically guilty?
- Medical conditions that affect field sobriety tests
- Can you refuse to perform FSTs?

The related articles widgets help the visitors spend more time, and build more appreciation for what you offer. They make you stand out when "being aggressive" won't. This is more likely to lead to a phone call to you.

#4: Make sure that the navigation is seamless and logical. It needs to make sense on your site so a visitor can look up and see immediately where they want to go, without getting trapped or lost in a certain area of your website.

If I'm on an article page, and I appreciate the writing, I want to be able to look up and see that attorney's profile. If I want to jump to another section, I can quickly click and go right there, irrespective of what page I'm on.

#5: Visitors want to see testimonials to build trust, and they must be able to find them instantly. Make your testimonials visible everywhere on your site so people get the reinforcement that you do a good job; that you're a good attorney and others have hired you and have had good outcomes.

Testimonials imply that YOU should hire this person – they speak very loudly in your defense.

#6: Phone number, email, physical address and office hours are <u>very important to be visible everywhere</u>. You never know where people will enter your site. One of the first and last things they will do once they decide that they need legal help is look for your phone number, address or email to contact you. Why make it hard for people to contact you? Why make them expend energy to search for your info?

So next time you pass a spider web in the office or eat a piece of Swiss cheese, think of your website; you'll think twice.

THE TWO MAIN DRIVERS
OF SEO SUCCESS

Make sure to review 'why getting on the 1st page of Google is a meaningless waste of time' and 'how a successful website looks like a spider web or gigantic wheel of Swiss cheese'.

For attorneys, a <u>successful</u> search engine optimization (SEO) has two main pillars: content and links.

To begin, Google now has made it such that ***<u>no one on earth can rush SEO results anymore</u>***. No one can get you on the first page of Google overnight. Getting 30, 50, or even 100+ unique visitors a day using SEO takes at least 6 months, and sometimes even a year.

➔ Anyone that promises quick page 1 ranking of Google is lying to you, plain and simple. ←

Google's algorithm has become so sophisticated, complicated and good at fighting spam that today Zeus himself couldn't rush the process.

Six to 12 months of SEO can bring your website to a 30-100 unique daily visitor level. This puts you in the range of having your phone ring multiple times a week or possibly every single day with potential clients.

Impatient attorneys often think, at this point: "Why bother? I don't have time for this. I don't want to wait 6-12 months!"

Why Bother Doing SEO, Long Term?

Think of SEO as getting yourself in cardiovascular shape – i.e. committing to regular gym workouts. SEO gives you long term benefits just like working out and building muscle and the good thing is that the results stay with you.

Unlike buying leads, running Google Adwords (pay per click), direct mail, banners, or other fast-response advertising, the day you stop SEO, you're not going to wake up the next day with no muscle tone and a cholesterol-clogged heart needing a quadruple bypass.

The moment you stop any of the above marketing methods or stop paying, the lights get shut off, and so do your phone and email leads. They are gone, like telling a stripper you have no money; gone without even so much as a smile.

On the other hand, a well-done SEO can stay with you for a long time, and even if you stop, the benefits do not fade instantly. I recommend that you do it forever, so long as you're profiting from it – i.e. you're making an ROI from your spend on it.

If the person doing SEO for you is doing their job properly, you'll experience an evolution from monthly expense, to break even to profit center in over 6-12 months.

When SEO is done right, it starts to pay for itself by attracting enough phone calls and emails from visitors to your website, (that you must still convert) to retained clients that pay you.

…As you continue building the SEO turns into a profit center, reliably getting you 4, 5, 6, maybe even 10 retained clients a month. Now the letters S-E-O **become ROI** and there's no reason to stop unless you don't understand basic math.

Does SEO Provide Quality Potential Clients or Just Tire Kickers and Time Wasters?

SEO is the carnival barker that gets the potentials to your website – into the tent and seated in front seats of the show. Unlike a salaried promoter, it's there to work for you day in and day out, continuously getting you clients.

You may ask: Why does SEO bring high-quality clients? The reason is because people have to SEARCH Google, Yahoo &/or Bing, and take initiative to find you. It doesn't sound like a tall hill to climb, but effort is effort – they have to chase you. It is not you chasing them with your advertising.

As you well know, potential clients have many questions. Nowadays, people 'Google' everything. It starts with the search – a list of websites comes up in search results. Each listing is, in fact, a tiny advertisement that looks like this:

<u>Arrested for Shoplifting in Paramus, NJ?</u>
<u>Call 201-555-1111</u>
www.nj-criminal-lawyer-smith.com/shoplifting
Don't think shoplifting is a 'no-big-deal' crime. A conviction may prevent you from being hired for several jobs. Call today.

Searchers very quickly scan the ads and click on one that catches their eye and piques their interest. Now the visitor is a potential that lands on your website. (Remember, they may not land on your homepage!)

What's next? The potential eyeballs your content – what's written, a picture or two, and decides within a few seconds if their search is matched and answered by what's displayed on your website.

If there is no match, there is no call and perhaps more searching. Failure to compel potentials to read more or call you results in a quick click of the back button which takes them back to search results and you've lost them, for now.

Can you now see all the effort and steps involved in someone **SEARCHING** for your information versus you advertising to them on TV, a bus stop, billboard, or other means?

A well-written, presented, and SEO'd website lies in wait; attracting visitors and compelling them to become educated and call you. This is why SEO-based visitors tend to be higher quality, potential clients. They have self-screened and only the more highly motivated ones will call or email.

Why Bother SEO'ing to Only Please Google? What About Yahoo, Bing, Ask, and the Other Search Engines?

You may be annoyed having to go through this whole rigmarole to please Google. However, Google does control over 80% of all searches. Would you rather focus on 20% of the pie vs. 80%? I didn't think so. Don't focus on Yahoo and Bing. Focus exclusively on Google and the other search engines will start showing your website, too. Sorry – it's time to let your dysfunctional love affair with Google Search begin.

What's The Process of "SEO'ing" a Website and Pleasing Almighty (God) Google?

The process starts with your mini ads that appear in Google search results (as I showed you previously). You should take the time to customize a compelling ad (called a title and meta description tag) for each page of your website as you build and add to it.

The goal of SEO is to optimize your website and make it 'Google friendly' or 'Google compliant'. There are myriad ways to do this. However, one way is to structure your site to guide visitors entering from any landing page to navigate quickly wherever they need to go on your site (i.e. no dead ends or rat holes where people can get stuck without an obvious way of getting out).

You also want to structure your site so that the people hitting a landing page are drawn further into the site, and compelled to click on at least one more page. This helps minimize the percentage of visitors bouncing off your site after just seeing one page. (Called "bounce rate" – an indicator of how engaging your site is in Google's eyes). Surprisingly, a good bounce rate is 50% for some pages and as high as 95% for others.

Always keep in mind that **your home page is not where** all visitors enter, as discussed in the Swiss cheese and spider web section. Remember, visitors come in through the windows, the basement, the side door and the attic of the website. They come in from every direction and on every possible page, depending on the content quality of that page. Shoplifting searches will land people on your shoplifting page. Sex crime searches will land people on those pages. General inquiries may go to your FAQ or homepage.

Without being exhaustive, here's more that you could do with your website: Set up Google maps, set up a sitemap, make sure you have terms and conditions and a disclaimer that by reading your site no attorney-client relationship is being created, and have a privacy policy.

All of these baseline, boilerplate things need to be done to make your site Google compliant.

The home-grown, mistake-inspired checklist, which I use on my attorney clients' behalf, has 80+ different line items to make sure that a website is ready and optimized to show up in Google.

Here's a good idea: As you talk to different SEO companies, ask to see their checklist for onsite optimization (i.e. the stuff they do to get a site ready to show up SEO-wise in Google).

Note: Want to see my 80+ item checklist? Email or call me and I'll gladly share.

Once you've done an on-site initial optimization –most of the work is up front and only requires a small amount of maintenance from then on – now we move to the heart of SEO.

The 2 Pillars of SEO – Content & Backlinks

The 2 pillars of SEO are content and links pointing to your site. Both are obtained continuously, at a somewhat steady pace over time.

Content is articles, relevant pictures, video, audio, and downloadable versions of the same, all that, which is posted on your website. Google searches on words, the presence of videos, pictures, and audio.

95%+ of Google relies on TEXT, so remember, content is vital, and words are king.

When you "google" something, you type in... WORDS.

When Google's algorithm pulls up relevant websites, you're now primarily looking at WORDS / TEXT. When a Googler clicks on a website, remember, every single page of a website can be landed on by a visitor, not just the home page.

What do searchers see when landing on your website? Your website's CONTENT - Words, pictures, videos, audio.

What Should Your Website's Content Look Like?

Imagine the typical criminal defense attorney's 20-page website that has cobwebs growing on it simply because it hasn't changed in years. None of the articles are new – the entire website is...static. These commonplace websites have the typical attorney profile page, a few pages of skeleton content, maybe a disclaimer, a contact us form, and not much else.

Now I want you to imagine that 90-pound weakling website shoved in the dirt by a 300-pound linebacker website made up of 300+ pages, containing 200 different articles on your various practice areas and the common questions and answers surrounding them.

A well-developed DUI website, for instance, would contain articles on DUI charges and consequences for 1st time and multiple offenders; common defenses; breath testing & refusals; field sobriety tests; driver's license suspension consequences;

post-conviction relief; probation types; lengths and violations; constitutional rights, victim impact panels, and more.

A broader criminal defense website would have articles on sex crimes; cybercrimes; robbery and assault; gun crimes; domestic violence; the different levels of misdemeanor versus felony crimes; juvenile criminal law; traffic offenses; theft crimes such as shoplifting, grand larceny and burglary; why hire a private attorney versus a public defender, and more.

I'll give you zero guesses which website, the weakling vs. the 6'5" linebacker, who will get the girls?

People 'google' thousands of different things daily, for millions of different questions that plague them.

Can a cobweb-covered, moldy cheese website left touched for a year have a snowball's chance in hell of getting those potentials?

...or will the active, growing, changing, content-filled, and developing website with 200+ articles on it get the visits?

Before You Complain About Writing 200+ Articles, Videos, and Creating Content...

Read the section on the Attorney-Author-Authority-Process. In it, I teach you how to effortlessly speak 7,000+ words an hour by phone and fill up your website almost completely with relevant online content in about nine, 1-hour-long sessions.

The 2nd Pillar of SEO – Links From 3rd Party Websites

A hyperlink ('link') is the blue, highlighted text with an underline, which on selection/click takes you to another web page or website entirely. The clickable words that make up a link are called the link's anchor text or link text.

In Google's eyes, this phenomenon works just like a high school popularity contest. Google favors more popular, more respected and more linked-to websites versus orphans. Other sites show respect and **give an implied recommendation** to visit your site by linking to it. At first glance, the  more links you have to your website sitting on 3rd party websites, the more popular and stronger your site will be. Additionally the more it will show up on the fabled 1st Page of Google results for a wider array of keywords.

Here come the twists. Anytime someone searches for something, Google seemingly, instantly sifts and sorts thousands of websites and decides which site to show at the top of the 1st page, which one 2nd, then 3rd, ad infinitum.

How does Google do this? There are over 200 factors baked into its algorithm. A MAJOR FACTOR is which sites have the most link popularity, and are therefore the most authoritative AND relevant to the subject being searched.

You'd be simplifying Google way too much to assume that the sites with the highest number of links and the most content will automatically be ranked 1st.

The prize of playing by Google's rules? Showing up at the top of page 1 for thousands and thousands of searches.

Soliciting and harvesting links is the 2nd pillar of SEO. Besides superior content, you want to get relevant, useful, quality links from other websites to show that your website is a worthwhile destination. Content without links gets you nowhere. Links without content get you nowhere.

In regards to links, don't think the more the merrier. In April-May 2012, Google slapped down millions of sites with their Panda and Penguin updates. They made it a lot harder for people to get credit for links that weren't "good", and resultantly many attorney websites lost ALL THEIR WEB TRAFFIC.

Here's how you judge if a link you want to get from another website to yours is worth asking for: The site has to be relevant to what you do, at least somewhat. Getting a link from a site about swimming pools is not going to be relevant to you as an attorney…Unless they have an article on their site about swimming pool injuries and you are a personal injury attorney. In that case, they would link to you from that article, and the link would make sense to a human reviewer and to Google's algorithm and you then get credit for it.

What kinds of sites and links meet the quality and relevance of Google standard? Another attorney's link to you would be a highly relevant and desired link. If it's a beer site and you are a DUI lawyer that may also be relevant. A true crime website is also highly relevant to you. If it's a financial website, it might be relevant and it might not. You have to assess and bridge the gap. You need to make sure your link makes sense, by, for instance, talking about the financial consequences of being arrested for a crime, losing your job or having a criminal record.

What Other Factors Make A Link Useful To You?

Make sure that the site linked to your website is authoritative and has been live on the web for a year or more - you absolutely don't want sites that were born yesterday. Older, more established sites are more authoritative and carry more credibility. Sites with many quality links to them, or obviously authoritative websites (an extreme example is the State Bar website or other legal organizations) are desirable.

A link from a newspaper or top-ranked attorney not in your field of practice is good to cultivate. The more authoritative the site linked to your website, the more SEO juice that link conveys and more traffic your site will attract from Google.

It's like a recommendation from your friend Joe versus a recommendation from the President of the United States. Which one conveys more authority to you? Which recommendation do you trust more highly? YES, Google's thoughts, exactly.

Factors That Can Improve or Hurt A Link

Run of Site Links - make sure when a site links to you, it doesn't link to you from every single page on that site – called a "run of site" link. Many folks mistakenly assume, "If a 100-page site links to me from every single page, I'll get 100 links."

No, it doesn't work that way. Only one or two-page site links from a given website give you "Link Juice/SEO Juice". The others are redundant and can actually hurt you. If Google sees that there are 100 links from the same site to you, they MAY devalue the link or hurt your search traffic because it makes no sense for a site to do this. It looks like spam and not true authority.

Link Text Keyword Stuffing / Redundancy - The link text itself, which is the blue underlined clickable text, can say different things. It can say "Click Here", or "Florida Criminal Defense Lawyer," or even "Learn about ABC Law Firm."

A lot of SEOs try to get the same link text over and over to your site. For example, let's say you want to be number one for "Los Angeles personal injury lawyer".

If every link the website gets says, "Los Angeles personal injury lawyer" or "Los Angeles personal attorney", Google knows it is way too coincidental that 50 different sites would link to your website using the same link text.

If you have 50 links, all with the same or similar link text, "Mistress Google" may crack her whip across your website's back and hurt your traffic.

You want to vary the link text while also ensuring that it makes sense, given the site it's coming from and the site it's linking to – i.e. your website.

Even if it's your name, the name of your firm, topic-based, like "Dallas Dog Bite Attorney" or "Click Here for More Info", all of those variations are expected and all are fine.

If a human being looks at your link profile or at any given link to your website, the acid test is: Does the link make sense or does it look like BS? If you pass the human viewer test and it makes sense, you will be fine.

Quality vs. Quantity Links – Who Wins?

Note: I paid $1,500 to the guy who does SEO for 1-800-Flowers.com, Inc. and the United States Patent and Trademark Office for a one day consult. He answered an important question: *"If you get one good, relevant, authoritative link, is that equivalent to ten or 100 crappy, non-relevant links?"*

He said, *"A good, relevant, authoritative link can be worth as much as 1,000 crappy, garbage, non-relevant links."*

Now you very well understand the stupidity of SEO firms that say, "We'll get you 500 links a month for $500". These guys are incentivized to get you as many garbage links as possible to fulfill their agreement to get you 500 links.

Even better, you can beat them by getting 3 relevant links a month to your site instead of 500 garbage ones.

I paid a lot of money to learn this and here I am giving this information to you for free in this book, <u>so pay attention</u>.

SEO Requires Patience

Sorry to rain on your parade, but it takes time and effort to find relevant links. You have to vet them to make sure that they benefit your site, not hurt it.

If you want to cut corners on content and links and still try to blast your site to the top of Google, you'll wake up sooner or later with zero Google traffic and a red, throbbing cheek where Google slapped you with a penalty that's  very difficult and time-consuming to undo.

I've received plenty of calls from attorneys that complain, "Oh my God. We had 100 visitors a day and now we have none. Google killed us. How do we fix this?"

Sorry buddy – when you anger the search engine gods, they unkindly and fiercely cut you down.

Even though content and links take time, they certainly don't take FOREVER. Focus on both for one year, check up on your website's progress and you'll prosper just like my attorney clients do.

The reward of daily phone calls from potential clients and a consistent, 4-10 retained clients a month means a home-run ROI on your SEO. Your website then becomes a big time asset that can bring you $100,000 a year or more in retention fees.

You now know WHAT to do, HOW to do it or at least monitor its progress, so don't be impatient. Spend the next 12 months building yourself an asset.

Social Media: Worth It For Law Firms or Over-Hyped Waste of Money?

Social media is a huge topic and has especially emerged in a massive way in the last five to seven years. Many law firms, just like any other business, are extremely interested in it. They want to know how effective social media actually is in getting leads and how to best use it.  There are innumerable companies out there that offer social media management, signifying the enormity of this industry. Unfortunately, I am here to somewhat rain on your parade and tell you that social media, in large part, is extremely difficult to work and to get results for law firms and for the legal industry.

Here's why: First of all, when I say social media, I mean YouTube, Facebook, Instagram, Pinterest, Periscope, Twitter and any number of other hundreds of social media applications out there.

Some of the reasons why this is a difficult medium is because when people are on social media, they are there to socialize, to make friends, to post pictures, to chat and that kind of thing. Your law firm advertisements or postings on social media, unfortunately, are therefore typically unwelcome because of the nature of what you talk about are legal problems and legal issues.

As you know, irrespective of your practice area is, when someone needs an attorney, it is generally for a negative issue. It is usually under circumstances that are fraught with concern and worry, have an unknown outcome, and an invariable expense. Think about it. Is a car accident a happy event? How about going through a divorce or a bankruptcy? What about being arrested for a crime, such as getting a DUI or getting a traffic ticket? How much fun is creating an estate plan because a loved one is dying? Civil lawsuits are extremely ugly. Intellectual property may not be negative initially but people are worried that they will not get their patron's information or they will not be able to get their copyrights and that sort of thing. If it is immigration, it can be extremely emotional. In those situations you may be waiting to hear if you can get a provisional waiver to get your wife or child to come live in the United States. You may even be facing deportation.

Unfortunately, almost everything the legal profession does except for perhaps adoption, (even that is fraught with worry and concern at times) is negative. Therefore, posting anything regarding your law firm on social media is inherently very difficult. You are bringing negativity to someone's attention and they have no interest in it unless they have a problem. If they have a problem, sure, then they would have an interest, but there is still definitely a reluctance to talk to an attorney or to hire an attorney through a social media platform. People perceive attorneys to be very stern, mean, unfriendly and expensive. People are embarrassed about their problems and are very skittish about engaging an attorney. They are full of fear of the court system, especially the criminal justice system.

The legal process involves people to personally disclose a lot of information. They may be deposed, cross-examined or they may have to pay a lot of money to defend themselves in a lawsuit or may have to file bankruptcies. As you can see, there is a lot of emotion wrapped up in legal issues to deal with.

Unfortunately, no matter how good a job you do for someone, after they become your client, once their case is over they hope to never see or hear from you again. You are associated with a negative time in their life; even if you helped them and even if you saved their lives. So what can you do? Is social media, which signifies positivity for people, worth it for attorneys?

Well, that answer really depends significantly on how you use it. There is a right way to use social media and a wrong way. First of all, I can tell you getting likes, followers, votes, pins on Pinterest and all of that stuff is a fake accomplishment. Likes do not put money in the bank or translate to client retention. Pins or reviews or any of that is pretty meaningless. It may show interest, it may not, but that is definitely not the metric to define your social media success or a failure. The question is, does this metric get you, clients? Does it make the phone ring with real potential clients, with real legal issues? Don't be seduced by anyone saying, "I can get you 10,000 followers on Facebook", or, "I can get you 3,000 views on YouTube".

These are just seductions and siren songs that waste your money and do absolutely nothing concrete to get you actual business and put money in the bank in a new trust account.

Then, there is a huge proliferation of websites: How do you even decide which websites to engage with? Well, I can tell you that just like with everything else, even though there are thousands of sites, there only are a few very select ones that could be useful to an attorney.

The top websites that I have seen that could be useful are YouTube, Facebook and Twitter. Beyond that, the usefulness of any social media site falls off like a stone. In fact I have found it incredibly rare that using any social media is really needed or does anything to get business for attorneys. Even amongst the big three mentioned above, it is still incredibly difficult and expensive to generate leads.

That being said, I am going to go into a little bit of detail on each and show you how they can potentially be used to help get you business. Of the top three forms of social media platforms, so far Facebook is actually number; YouTube I would say is second and third is Twitter in terms of generating business for attorneys.

There are a couple of common mistakes that attorneys make when utilizing social media. One is that social media cannot be tracked so it is  difficult to tell if it is generating actual business through actual leads. You definitely want to use things like tracking phone numbers, special landing pages or websites and ads that are very narrowly focused on a core demographic. These focused and directed methods will help to ensure that you are targeting the right people and that you are not randomly blasting too wide of an audience.

Another aspect to consider is your offer: Now, what does not work at all on social media platforms is your standard run-of-the-mill 'Call us for a free consult' ad. Because of the sale oriented negativity associated with it and the fear people have that this information is being used to serve them ads, on some social media platforms it is not even allowed. You have to be careful with that.

What will work is providing useful, helpful information with a call to action such as, "Call us for more information about X", at the end of your video. Eighty percent of your article should be pure qualitative information - useful to the potential client. Some examples could be to a cheat-sheet on how to get through a bankruptcy or on how to survive divorce and not lose everything or how to get compensation if you are injured. These kinds of soft offers, information, reports or cheat-sheets, tend to work far better than standard commercials on social media. Again, it could be an article, a pdf, a cheat-sheet, a video or you can even have a landing page on your website that shows a video and a free download; all combinations of these work. They are all different, but they can all work.

Let me go into the specific platforms: I am going to start from the bottom with Twitter. Twitter allows you to post tweets, links to videos, audios and free reports. Twitter can work in favor of an attorney. You have to make a Twitter account and start getting followers and follow other people that are possible influencers for your targeted potential clients. Twitter has an advertising platform where you can advertise to people based on their feed conversation.

For example, people that are talking about a car accident may be injury clients. People that are talking about DUI classes, drinking or bars are good potential DUI clients. People talking about family issues and that kind of thing may have a divorce case. You can target people on Twitter based on parameters like hashtags, interests, who they follow, who is following them, and more. It is definitely not easy to do and really requires a social media specialist to get into it, but Twitter can be a source for some leads.

Next, let's go over YouTube: YouTube is definitely a great resource. You may not even have to pay to advertise there. As we talked about in other parts of this book, a  great thing to do is to record a series of one-question-one-answer videos, one to three minutes long and answer a legal question. The image of the video on YouTube can either be you as a talking head at your desk or it could be just an audio with a still image of you on it listing your firm name, website, phone number etcetera; thus the video can take several forms. It does not have to necessarily be a talking head and the quality does not have to be top notch. The information, however, has to be straight to the point, useful and relevant. My suggestion is that you get at least 100 YouTube videos up on the web over the course of a year. You can add them at a regular pace of several videos a month in order to stay relevant, thereby consistently growing the possible audience that can find you on YouTube.

Now, you can also advertise your videos. Have you ever noticed that on YouTube, when you watch a video, an ad comes up in the first five seconds? After five seconds or thirty seconds, you can skip the ad? Or when you are watching a video, it shows related videos in the top right? There are several spots to advertise on YouTube in several different ways. Depending on which videos you advertise on YouTube, you may have relevant traffic or not. In some cases, you may even be able to advertise on top of your competition. You can also advertise based on interest, channels that people are subscribed to, age, gender, and many other factors. Targeting on YouTube is getting more and more sophisticated, and again, it is very easy to get the simple videos done and uploaded. Therefore, YouTube is a good platform to reach potentials.

If you did not know this, YouTube is searched billions of times a day. It's the world's second largest search engine and is the biggest program for searches of videos. It's definitely a spot that you may want to consider advertising on and the costs right now are relatively low because it is a new media.

Lastly, I will discuss Facebook with you:

Facebook has recently cracked down and made it difficult to advertise; but it still can work for you. I recommend that your law firm definitely have **facebook**

its own page on Facebook. More importantly, you need a Facebook page so that you can advertise. I am sure you have seen ads on the right side of your page and ads in your newsfeed. Again, just like the other social media, you do not want to directly say, "Have you been arrested for such and such?"

You're not allowed to even say things like, "Are you facing bankruptcy?" You need a softer approach such as, "Are you curious about what filing bankruptcy can do?" or "Are you curious about how to get through a divorce?" and that kind of thing. Your offer has to be softer and again include a free report, a video, a download, even a free consultation, but something that provides information first. Otherwise, Facebook will not even show your ads.

Now, Facebook advertising, again, can be written or it can be video. The video, right now on Facebook is incredibly cheap. We are finding that people can get views for five to ten cents, sometimes less, so it is definitely a great way to get a video seen and get people to take action. We get leads from Facebook and it is possible for attorneys to do the same. Although again, people are there to socialize, so it is quite difficult. One very unique thing about Facebook is it is targeted – they have teamed up with a lot of top data gathering companies like Axiom and Melissa Data. Therefore you are able to target people in many different ways on Facebook. For instance, you can target people in a ten-mile radius around your office who are female, 45-60 years of age, who are interested in a second home, children or family, who are facing marital problems, and who have a net worth of $100,000 or more. With Facebook, you can get pretty sophisticated and precise in your targeting. That is going to be necessary in order for you to have an effective ad which is reached, accessed and seen by the right people or potentials.

There is a lot to go into on Facebook and you really need a specialist to work on it for you. I cannot go into all of that in this book. What I can tell you is there is a nice add-on presently on Facebook. The best way I found to use Facebook is  similar to sending a newsletter to past clients or a newsletter to potential future clients. Offer valuable information, but offer new information once a week. You cannot run the same ad forever. Run a fresh ad with a different piece of information each week and treat it like a newsletter that goes out to people of a certain demographic, in a certain radius of certain targeting. If it drips on them week after week, month after month, people get interested and engaged. Facebook may not even be an immediate result. It may take several months of campaigns and a modest budget in order to start getting responses, similar to the newsletter responses. However, that is a far better way to use it.

One great feature Facebook has is, if you have a person's name and phone number or email address, you can upload a list to the site and it will match as many of those people as it can with those that have Facebook accounts and allow you to advertise to them. For example, let's say you have a list of emails of past clients and you upload that to Facebook. You can create what is called the "custom audience" and advertise to those people on the site. This is a great and cheap way to reach them if you cannot do so in any other way. For any potential client that calls your office, whether they hire you or not, you should get their name and email, or get their phone number and add them to your list and continue to advertise or follow-up with them on Facebook. Stick with this routine.

Every time you come into contact with anyone that can potentially have a legal situation or refer you to someone who does, add them. I have seen attorneys build up a list of several thousand people that regularly hear from them and give them quite a few referrals. That is why Facebook is the most powerful social media outlet right now and these are just some of the ways in which it can be used.

That is a recap on how social media can be used to reach potential clients. Typical budgets for social media do not have to be very high. You can get by with $100 to $200 a month. Some of the bigger budgets I have seen could be as much as $500 a month. Typically though, it is quite a bit cheaper than Google Pay-per-click and it can be very effective, especially if used over time and with patience.

LIVE CHAT: SQUEEZING OUT 10% MORE LEADS

What is a live chat and what is its usefulness?

Have you ever been to a website and noticed a box or dropdown appear from the top of the screen or wiggle and say, "Operators are standing by. Chat with us now!"?

That is what is referred to as live chat. There are several services I know that provide this feature. One is Apex, the other one is Ngage. Additionally we, as part of Speakeasy Marketing, provide live chat to our clients.

So is live chat useful or not? Well, during testing with the use of Heat Maps (which show where actual users click on a website), we see a couple of things. Often when the live chat box opens up on a website, the visitor will be asked, "Do you want to chat right now?" Then the visitor needs to click 'yes' or 'no'.

A lot of people do click 'No', but as soon as they do that, they see the regular website page they landed on and they can browse or do whatever they need to do. In our experience, we have not seen that live chat annoys people or pushes them away. There are ways to do it effectively versus not effectively.

Here are a couple of recommendations on how to do it the right way and make it effective:

You choose whether the live chat box will appear immediately when a visitor arrives to a website or whether it will appear after ten seconds or thirty seconds or after a one minute delay, etc. In our experience, we find that it is best for it to appear after a twenty-second delay. If someone spends twenty seconds on the page, it means that they are at least somewhat engaged. By that point, they could be reading the article and finding out if it is telling them what they want to know and the live chat box can appear at that time.

Another recommendation is once the live chat box appears and someone else navigates to a new page, don't have it appear again, rather have it sit on the side of the page. Let's say someone is on a smartphone (mobile enabled website), don't have a box covering up the text. You can still have a tab on the side where something may be wiggling in the corner that says "Live Chat". That way the person can navigate the site and consume other information, but not have the live chat box popping up every time they go to another page.

Another possible way to handle this is to customize the live chat window. People often use stock photos of a woman with headphones. Some of the smarter firms will use a picture of one or more of the attorneys at the firm. This gives the appearance that it is customized and the live chat is integrated with the firm, which is important from a client perspective. It creates more trust if the actual attorneys themselves show up in the chat window and this way, you can customize what is said.

Typically the live chat box says, "Need Help - Chat with us now!"

However, we have also successfully tested, "Have a question about your legal situation? Click yes to chat now!"

The bottom line is that you can customize and have the chat box say different things.

There is another service that is somewhat similar and is called OptiMonk. It throws up a box that is like live chat, but it's actually an exit pop. It's a window that appears and you can either set it to appear after a live chat or instead of live chat when people are about to leave the website.  We have tested those as well and they do work to get leads. They can also make an offer to download your free guide to "Surviving Divorce", "Filing Bankruptcy or "Avoiding a DUI Conviction", for example.

It can ask people if they got the answers they wanted to the question they had or it could ask people if they would like to do a free consult by phone or by email. These live chats, OptiMonk, and similar services usually are pretty inexpensive as well. They will run anywhere from $25 a lead on down to a flat fee or monthly plan of $200 to $300 a month. They are well worth it.

You may ask: "Are they going to grow the lead volume tremendously?" No. However, in our experience, they will probably add five to ten percent additional leads a month. That means one extra lead every other month, so again, this service is worth it.

Here are a few more issues regarding live chat: You must decide when you will have the service manned. Will it be 24x7/365 or will it just be the business hours, 7 am to 7 pm? We have seen that ninety-five percent of leads come in during business hours on the weekdays. People tend to assume that attorney's offices will only be open on weekdays and not always on weekends or late nights. Therefore, typically having the live chat answered, 7 am to 7 pm in your time zone is just fine. If you want to be really diligent about it, you can always have your answering service answer the live chats and if they will do that, you can then integrate it 24x7/365. Of course, that is somewhat better, but marginally so and in my experience, you do not really need it.

Another imperative question is who answers the live chat? This is important because you want to have a script ready for that person. You want someone, if possible, that can engage with the potential, but not provide legal advice; instead act as an effective handler of the chat. You do not want someone that is not from the United States, if possible, because he or she may provide answers that do not translate well. For example, someone may say, "I'm considering getting a divorce", or, "How much is it for a bankruptcy?", and the live chat person will say, "Are you in need of legal help?"

The caller just said, "I need help with my bankruptcy," and may then describe their case and the live chat person will say, "That's wonderful to hear. How may I help you?"

I have seen these responses and they make no sense to the potential on the other end. The potential will then just click away because they know the person is from a third world country and not credible legal help.

Another issue is getting the live chat box answered quickly when people type in questions and information. You want to make sure that the service you pick is answering the live chats and not chatting with ten to twenty people at a time. That will slow down response time to the point where most people will abandon the chat.

Additionally, it is helpful to make sure to get the person's email, phone number, name, and relevant information about their case in the live chat so that you can follow up. If you do not get this data, the chat is worthless so it is very important to do so. Again, using scripts is critical. Here is a very simple script that we use that will be very effective for you:

"Hi, this is the law firm of ABC. My name is Suzan. What legal questions do you have today?"

The potential will chat, "Oh, I was in an accident. I was rear-ended and my neck hurts. Do I need a lawyer for this kind of thing?"

The standard stock answer is "Tell me a little bit more about your case and then I'll direct you to the right person".

The person chatting will then give details about the case and the response from your live chat person respond should be, "Oh my goodness, that's terrible", or, "Okay, I've got it. Tell me more," followed by, "Based on what you've told me, you want to talk to Attorney Smith. He or she is the best one that will be able to answer your legal questions. Let me get your information and I will connect you now to get help by phone or by email".

That is a simple script that works very well. It shows empathy, gathers information for follow-up and is probably one of the best live chat scripts that you can use. You do not need to get fancy and, of course, you do not want the reps practicing law or giving too much information. However, they do need to get some basic details and it can be very helpful.

Now, in terms of follow up, how soon should you do so on live chats? The answer is immediately or as soon as possible. In other places, I have talked about the IBM study of the 'golden hour', which says that conversion to leads dropped off dramatically after five minutes, ten minutes, fifteen minutes, and then an hour. After that, the conversion was horrible because people would have moved on by that point to talk to another attorney. To avoid this scenario, you want to have the transcription of these chats forwarded to you immediately. If possible, have it texted to you or someone in your office to be notified so they can engage with the live chat immediately as it is still live or at worst, respond to the chat within minutes. Again, it is not a perfect situation, but this can help add five or ten percent to your lead flow. The more traffic you get to your site the better.

Now, one last thing about live chat: Once you have this information, if the person does not answer you when you email them or call them, do not give up and wait for them to contact you again.

Follow up! I want to refer you to my follow up section where we have handcrafted emails and voicemails to follow up in a predictive way with potential clients. Do not just simply give up on them. These leads are just like any other leads you get. Always follow up!

One last thing to note is that live chat should be installed on every single page of your website; not just the homepage. As you may remember, Google can direct visitors to any page of your site to land on, not just the homepage.

Snail Mail (aka Direct Mail or Jailer Mailer) – YES, It CAN Get You More Retained Clients

Direct mail is literally getting an envelope and a stamp, putting a letter inside and mailing it through the U.S. Post Office, UPS or FedEx. Direct mail is also called "jail mail" or "snail mail".

In the present world of social media fanaticism, the "ancient tradition" of sending a letter in the mail is very effective. Did you realize that statistics say 65% of people hate getting e-mail and are completely overwhelmed by it?

No doubt you can't stand spam and you're in good company because **94% of all e-mail sent is SPAM**. Not sure about you, but that amazes me to think what it would be like if spam ceased to exist... Ahhhh…

On the contrary, 63% of people say that they enjoy getting direct mail. They enjoy the experience of opening their mail, of getting a postcard, or especially, a package.

Remember how you felt years ago when your grandparents sent you a Christmas card with money or even a care package?

A letter or package can be delightful or frightful. At the end of the day, either way, it causes a big-time emotional response THAT only few other marketing methods can do.

Unless you're getting the registered mail or an obvious bill, sorting through your mail can be an enjoyable experience, driven by curiosity.

Paper Mail Creates an Intimate Experience

Once you open a letter, it becomes a one-on-one experience at an emotional and physical level. You're opening an envelope with your hands – it's a physical experience. You instinctively hold your breath for a moment until the envelope opens and you see what's inside. This experience is exclusive and undivided.

There are no Twitter or Facebook pop-ups. There is no way to click back to another 25 websites. There are no ads and none of the other 99 distractions you find on the internet.

How many windows do you have open on your computer from various web pages? Have you ever visited a web page and forgot why you even went to it? Ever shake your head in frustration that you have a hard time paying attention to ANYTHING on the internet?

Compare that feeling to reading a paper letter sitting back on your couch. It feels like a bubble is surrounding you and the letter you're reading and the outside worlds' sounds and events are shut out, if only for a minute.

How You Can Wield Direct Mail to Clobber Your Competitors

Ok, so now that you feel the romance of direct mail, how is this <u>useful to you as an attorney</u>? Who wants to hear from YOU, an ATTORNEY? Yuck, right?

My favorite direct mail data guy, Mark, has been providing me the names, home addresses, and charges of people recently arrested near to you for the past 8 years. His experience shows: **70% of criminal defense clients will <u>procrastinate until</u> 5 days or less before their court date**.

I bet you are thinking, "If you don't get 'em on the first or second day, I'll never retain. They've all hired someone else by then."

NOT TRUE.

Ask the man who has sent out 50,000 letters a month for the past 96 months, what REALLY HAPPENS out there.

Moral of the story? If you're only hitting up potential clients the first 1-5 days, and then giving up, **_you're missing out_** on 70% of the possible people that would otherwise retain you!!!

More chilling facts about attorney direct mail, if you're smart enough even to use it in the first place:

97% of mail sent by attorneys goes out one time ONLY, and the same day they get their potential client data.

Do you send multiple letters? Stats say only 3% attorneys do, because most folks mistakenly think 2nd, 3rd or 4th letters are not only "too expensive", but that everyone's already retained an attorney by then and it's too late.

Choose: Would you rather get 30% of the pie with a one time, day one mailer, or 100% of the pie with a 3-step mail sequence sent out over 1, 2 or 4 weeks?

There's huge opportunity in direct mail to get clients. I'm currently running direct mail for several attorney-clients.

One guy received <u>21 calls</u> and <u>retained 6 clients</u> his first month of doing this! **He spent $3,500 (because NY is the most expensive state to do it in, of course) and took in $18,400 in gross retainer fees.** NOT BAD, huh?

I've had to wrestle most lawyers to the ground to get them to try it, (ensuring their mail is State Bar-compliant). The results speak for themselves.

Supercharging Your Direct Mail Results

Most attorneys are afraid to even try direct mail, much less "push the envelope" (bad pun) to maximize its return on investment.

In some cases, a plain letter in a white envelope with a stamp will serve you well. However, there's a heck of a lot of tweaking, tracking and testing that you have to do to (and should WANT to do) in order to push your results from 3x your money to possibly 10x your money or even more.

How People Sort Their Mail

Do you realize that people sort their mail over the garbage can, mentally making a "keeper" pile of interesting stuff that must be opened now, the second pile of essentials, like bills, and are tossing the rest?

The first things to get opened and read are the items that people think are personal, interesting, or evoke curiosity. The other stuff is obvious junk that goes straight into the garbage can. **You have to survive this initial sort.**

To make matters more difficult, some people have a gatekeeper (if they're getting mail at work vs. home). Even at home someone's spouse or child may throw away your letter if it looks like junk or it's obviously a solicitation. Surviving the initial sort is not an easy task and letters, no matter how fascinating or needed, are often thrown away, unopened.

If They Don't Read Your Masterpiece, What's the Point?

You can't just assume that your mail will be opened and read. If you send out 100 letters this week, don't dare assume "I'm sending 100 letters and 100 people will read them".

If you're in a competitive area where 50 other attorneys are mailing the same person, all using white envelopes with the name of a law office on each,

Why Would They Ever Open <u>Your Letter</u>?

The most extreme example I've seen of this is in Los Angeles. There are literally 100 different attorneys using 'direct mailing' for criminal cases. There are guys doing really well but believe me, they're NOT just sending run-of-the-mill white envelopes. There's a lot more to direct mail than what meets the eye.

You have to go out of your way to differentiate what you send to ensure direct mail works for you.

How can you increase the likelihood of someone opening and read your mail? Try using "grabbers" – small items you put into your mail piece that give it a 3D effect.

For instance, I've used a small bag of shredded money, a compass, a little toy soldier, a rock, and all kinds of small objects to make the mail I send out **lumpy**.

When someone gets an envelope that's bulging with an object inside, natural curiosity will lead them to open and read it - and that's the whole point.

Get your mail OPENED and then READ.

Don't just throw something weird inside but tie it into your letter itself.

Let's say you throw in a miniature hourglass (30 cents each) and reference the object in your letter by saying, "Time may be running out on your criminal case."

You're referencing the grabber, the envelope is lumpy and 3D, and the whole package makes sense to the recipient. It may even make them smile.

A higher open rate, curiosity, and a unique angle will improve your direct mail results dramatically.

Another way to differentiate your snail mail is to hand-write on the envelope or put testimonials in with your letter. You can send an oversized envelope, or send by tube mailers.

Did you know you can literally mail a 6" tall, big pill bottle or a bank bag? Imagine your potential clients getting a zippered, canvas purse in which you'd normally put money and take it to the bank with your letter inside or a gigantic pill bottle, with your prescription for legal help.

I bet you'll get nearly 100% of people to open it.

Do you know what happens when someone gets these items in the mail? They look at it and think, "What the heck is this thing and who sent me **THIS?**"…

…and they OPEN IT. Once you achieve this, you've got a fighting chance for them to read it and call you.

Direct mail DOES work. Don't be afraid of trying unusual mailings like my suggestions here. It's worth the small extra expense to get far more readership, calls, and RETAINED CLIENTS.

Don't let "cost" hold you back.

<u>The only thing that matters is ROI.</u> (Return on investment).

Suppose you spend $1 per person for your boring, "me-too" white envelope mailer:

<u>Results:</u> You spend $2,000 a month in the direct mail at $1 per letter mailed (2,000 letters sent). One in 100 people call, and 1 in 4 calls retain you. At $1 per mailer, you're paying $100 to get a phone call and $400 to get a retained client. An average client pays a $1,000 retainer.

Your ROI is: ($1,000 * 5 clients) / $2,000 spent = 250%

Expensive? Let's compare.

Scenario 2: You wipe away your tears and fears and use a pill bottle with a letter inside. You spend $2,000 a month, but this time, at *$3.50 per mailer* and you send out only 571 letters versus 2,000 letters.

This time, 1 in 20 people call you, and you retain 1 in 4.

You retain 7 clients (rounding down) at $1,000 each, making your ROI: ($1,000 * 7 clients) / ($2,000 spent) = 350%.

Which one is more "expensive?"
Which one is more effective?

> Would you rather spend $2,000 to get $5,000,
> or spend $2,000 to get $7,000?

DIRECT MAIL DOUBTS – DISPELLING MISCONCEPTIONS

Direct Mail sounds great but is greatly feared by attorneys.

"My State Bar won't allow me to do that."

Have you really checked on the actual rules in your state?

Many states DO allow direct mail, as long as it satisfies some easy State Bar requirements regarding disclosures, and disclaimers.

Some of the common rules I've seen are that it has to say "Attorney Advertisement" in a certain large font at the top of the letter. No problem. Be compliant, but don't be afraid.

Another common rule requires the mandatory disclaimer: "If you've already found legal counsel, please disregard this letter."

No problem. You can write that. Don't assume, "I can't do it."

Have you heard this misconception? - "Direct mail only gets you crappy clients with no money or tire kickers."

Not true. You can get really good clients from direct mail if you're mailing for DUI or other specific offenses.

If you're only mailing for traffic tickets, well then what do you expect to get?

Some of my attorney clients have gotten $10,000 cases from direct mail. An unfounded assumption will only make you miss out on this opportunity to get clients.

Assumptions can cripple you:

"People don't read nowadays. It's all internet-based."

Interested people DO read compelling and relevant information that helps them. When they get a well-written direct mail piece that is individually and specifically relevant to them, you would be surprised who comes out of the woodwork and calls you to retain. It's all walks of life; believe me.

"Direct mail doesn't work. I've tried it before."

"There's too much competition."

Yes, in some major metros, there IS INDEED A LOT of competition, but you CAN find a niche and succeed and profit from your spend. If you send a plain white envelope with a boring letter without grabbers, different envelopes, stamps, or testimonials- then sure – your competition will stomp all over you and you'll lose money.

However, if you work at it, direct mail is a very powerful way to get clients. I don't care how much competition there is. I did a mailer for an attorney in Los Angeles where there are literally 100 people competing and mailing, and he got plenty of responses and profited from the effort. If it can be done there, it can be done anywhere. Trust me.

"Direct mail is unprofessional;"

"I'm bothering people by sending them mail;"

Ok, you can choose to starve to death because you're assuming that people who respond to a letter in the mail don't really need help and would be "offended". Other guys who DO direct mail will happily eat your lunch, dinner, and tomorrow's breakfast.

"What will other attorneys think of me?"

Do you really care? Do you think other attorneys' opinions have any bearing on whether you go broke, feed your family, or have retained 10 clients last month versus two the month before? Worry about yourself. Everyone else is busy doing the same thing.

Below the Radar and in the Dark

One cool thing about direct mail is it operates below the radar and in the dark. Unless another attorney sees your letter, or if a client has brought it in for some reason, most attorneys have no idea what you're doing in direct mail. Sure, they will start to see you in court a lot and wonder what your secret is, but that makes it all the better, doesn't it?

On the internet everything you do ends up on YouTube, Facebook or Google search results. On the internet, everything can be copied at light speed.

Direct mail is success through stealth.

IF REFERRALS ARE THE BEST CLIENTS, WHY AREN'T YOU FOCUSED ON GETTING MORE OF THEM?

I'm sure you do get referrals from past clients, yes? And when you do, I'd bet they're the best clients. Not only because they are "free" to retain, but they're probably the best-behaved clients as well. You don't have to do 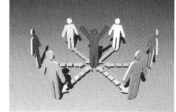 much work or put in much effort to convince them to retain you because they're **"pre-sold"**.

I'm sure you smile to yourself when someone calls and says, "My friend / neighbor / father / mother / cousin / whoever referred me to you."

Referrals are the best kind of client because they're less resistant to price, they are more willing to work with you and are less resistant to what you tell them.

So if referrals are so good, why aren't you
focusing on getting more of them?

Here are the voices inside many attorneys' heads when asked about generating more referrals:

> *"If I ask my past clients to refer me, I'm bothering them.*
> *I already get referrals.*
> *I'm not going to get any more by bothering these people."*

Let me tell you from personal experience, if done properly, this won't be true in the least.

Yes, I understand that if you're a criminal defense attorney, your past clients may hope to never hear from you again…

…but what they are actually hoping to never hear about is their past criminal case.

Your past clients have now moved on with their lives, and they're certainly okay to hear about the general topics of interest that they may enjoy in their normal lives.

We will get into how you can communicate with them on topics that are outside the law – about general things they enjoy. **Then they won't mind** hearing your name again and again; especially if you got positive results in their case and you have interesting, useful information to impart to them.

Why Focus On Getting Referrals? Is it Worth It?

You're probably already investing thousands a month on Yellow Pages, SEO, Google pay-per-click, direct mail, TV, radio, billboards, Facebook, Twitter, or some other marketing fad of the day.

Now, it's time to redirect a tiny portion of that money to getting more referrals.

Before I explain HOW, check out the story of a vehicle accident attorney from Vancouver Canada who gets 77% of all his new clients from past client referrals.

This blew me away when I heard it, and I couldn't believe it.

This guy sends a physical paper and ink, monthly newsletter to all his past clients. He has been doing this for years and told me it really doesn't cost that much to do.

Over the years he consistently adds past clients to the list, and he swears he gets plenty of calls from these people. People even call to say: "I love your newsletter. It's interesting. My friend Joe was in a car accident and I thought of you, so I told him to call you."

With 77% of his business coming from past client referrals, this attorney is pretty happy because he doesn't need to blow thousands of dollars on various other marketing efforts.

He already has a great resource of people sending him clients. It's fantastic and definitely do-able if you work at it.

Here's how you can copy his success: Send all your past clients a monthly printed newsletter by post office mail; **not just email.** It has to be a physical, paper and ink mailer, which is sent once a month; not every 6 months or once a year.

If this sounds daunting to you, let me make it a little easier for you.

Start with your most recent, past clients until you reach ones that have been gone for up to two years. You may ask me – "Why?" Because up to two years, many people are still living at the same address.

Two years of past clients will give you enough of a starting base to contact a fair number of past clients successfully. The average solo practitioner that I've seen gets about 85 clients a year. If you take the past two years, you have a solid base of 170+ past clients to work from.

So how much does it cost to keep your name in front of these people? Let's say you have 200 names and the average cost to send a newsletter is $1.50 / person / month, including postage. Spend $300 per month to **communicate 12x a year with 200 of your past, happy clients? It's a no-brainer.**

To keep your list clean and effective, make sure to periodically filter it. Add new clients as you complete their cases and remove ones that no longer have valid addresses or come back as returns.

Let's look at the numbers: $300 a month x 12 = $3,600 a year to mail to your list. One referral case every 3 months, (at $1,200 a case) means you'll at least break even.

Keep up your mailer consistently, and you'll retain quite a bit more as with time, your newsletters' visibility and stickiness in peoples' memories improves.

It's a cost-effective way to keep in contact with your list, keep your name in front of them, and get referrals. It pays for itself pretty darn quick and makes you money.

Why and How Does a Monthly Newsletter to Past Clients Work?

For instance, your past client, John Smith, is not an orphan. He might have a wife and kids. Maybe his parents are alive and he has sisters, brothers, cousins, people at work and people he knows in his social circles through Facebook.

Let's say you represented John Smith a year ago on a DUI case, and you got his charges reduced, helped him avoid jail, and he's happy with your legal representation.

Now John starts getting your monthly newsletter and at first, nothing happens. After three months of getting your newsletter, he's used to getting and seeing it come in the mail. He's even glanced through it a couple of times, and your name comes to mind when he gets the mail, thinking, "Huh. There's Attorney X's monthly mailer. Cool."

Nothing happens, but after about four months of getting your newsletter, John's cousin, Joe Blow, gets into a fight with his girlfriend. The fight gets loud and police are called.

Joe Blow is arrested and charged with domestic violence. He is freaking out and ends up on John's couch because there is an order of protection and he can't go home.

Joe: *"Man what am I going to do? You know any lawyers I can talk to? "*

John: *"Remember my DUI a while back? My guy XYZ helped me out. He sends me this letter in the mail each month and it's got his name on it. Let me look… Ok, here it is. Call him. He can help you out like he did for me."*

Voila! Joe Blow calls you as a referral. Without that paper newsletter, your past client might've easily said, "I had this guy who helped me out, but I don't remember his name. I…uh… think it was… Never mind. Just Google it and you'll get someone." Joe may google but he'll also be distracted by other attorney's information, while a newsletter will give him undivided exposure to you.

Which situation is going to get you business without you having to go hunting for it? Would you rather have your name in front of your past clients or have them forget about you, which, **believe me**, happens all the time.

➔   A monthly newsletter to past clients <u>works</u>.

What should your newsletter contain? Remember, it should not be about legal issues because people don't want to hear about that scary stuff.

You may be thinking, "I'm too busy for this."

I know you're extremely busy in court, dealing with all kinds of issues and preparing for trial. The idea of writing a whole newsletter each month and sending it out yourself?

"Ain't gonna happen" - I get it.

Don't worry – I have an easy way where you don't have to write a single word. You don't even have to mail it out yourself. There are automated solutions and templates with all the interesting articles that you need in them.

Even if you don't have time, you can still get a professional looking, informative and interesting newsletter out the door monthly with zero effort on your part.

No Work? Let Me Explain How It's Possible.

Instead of a boring, law-filled, scary newsletter, the key is to make it in a mini-Reader's Digest format. I have access to multiple services that provide a template for articles that change monthly, including things like a recipe from a famous cook, a crossword puzzle, Sudoku or word jumble.

Also included will be several articles about current events, a celebrity, and a historical figure. Additionally is an article about what's going on this month. (ex: February is Black History Month, so the newsletter template would contain an article on a famous black person in history)

It WOULD be ideal to include in the package at least one article that talked about you and things in your personal life you're willing to disclose.

Let's say you're an avid golfer. You may want to include an article this month about your golfing experiences. Next month an article about your son's baseball team success. The month after that, it may be a trip you took your family on to Disney.

Even with one personal article, your newsletter is still 90% template. At worst, you may want to carve out 15 minutes a month to personalize your newsletter further with an article.

The initial setup is only where all the work comes in, and it takes barely 30 minutes. You want to have your law firm's name, your name, your picture, address, phone number, email, and a short call to action:

> *"Call me anytime for legal help. I'm ready to step in and help you again as I've helped you in the past."*

Why Would Anyone Waste Their Time Reading MY Newsletter?

Millions of people read and regularly subscribe to the Reader's Digest. My wife subscribes and I've found myself sitting in the bathroom, reading an article or two. It has human interest stories, tips on saving money, surprising research, a crossword, and all kinds of generically appealing information.

I enjoy getting it and so have millions of people over the past 50 years, and if your newsletter is similar, guess what?

Surely your past clients will read and enjoy it.

The newsletter, done right, has mass appeal. It's not pushy – it's informative, interesting, non-threatening, entertaining, and so **IT GETS READ**.

Unbeknownst to your past clients, its secret mission is to build a recall value; to keep your name in front of your past clients without boring or scaring them with legal issues.

Sadly, although it's a simple process and totally automated, nowadays most attorneys are unwilling or afraid to do these newsletters...

<u>Here are some lame excuses I've heard:</u>

1. "It costs too much": Let me tell you, $1.50 per month, per person is ridiculously cheap. There is no cheaper form of communication than that.

Your mailer is 100% targeted and is highly effective. The ROI can be off the charts, and it blows away any result you'd ever get from generic ads in magazines, newspapers, pay per click, or website visitors.

2. "I don't have the time": Even if you don't want to write a single word, there are services that can help. I'll even help you set up the newsletter the first time or you can use a provider that will do it for you.

For a pathetically small fee of about $80 a month, many available services will populate the newsletter with new, current, topical articles each month.

Also, you don't even have to mail it out – a newsletter service will even do THAT for you. Push a button, and out it goes.

3. "It's a lot of work to get my past client list together": Have your admin do it. Maybe she'll curse your name for a few days, but once it's done, it's a valuable database for business promotion. Now you're off to the races. Every time you get a new client, just add them to the list. If you get 10 new clients a month, it will take you one minute per client to add them to your list. (10/month * 12 = 120 additional subscribers)

4. **"I don't know what to write":** Again, there are "done for you" solutions. You don't have to write.

5. **"No one's going to read this junk":** We talked about this. The Reader's Digest model works.

6. **"Can I just mail it once a year or every six months instead of every month?"** : Once every six months or one time a year isn't enough for positive results. Stop being a cheapskate, and don't worry that you're "bothering people". You're NOT. Once a month is a sweet spot – rare enough that it doesn't harass the person, yet frequently enough so they remember you.

   After someone's received and eyeballed three, four or five newsletters, they know that every month they will get one from you and will actually **look forward to getting it**.

   You'll stay in their minds and it's highly likely that there are lingering copies sitting around the house. Being able to grab it and hand it to a friend, co-worker, or family member in need beats sending them to the Google jungle, only to be suckered away by competition.

7. **"I don't want to bother people"** - Stats show that well over 60% of people **_enjoy_** getting direct mail, unlike email, which is literally 94% SPAM.

   Getting something in the mail is like a gift. This gift of the newsletter may be four pages back to front. It doesn't take long to read. All the content is enjoyable. You can sit for five minutes and read it. It works very well.

8. **"Can I just email it instead of going through the hassle of direct mailing it?"** - You can, but SHOULD **NOT**. Direct mail exudes a lot more power than just email. Physically getting something in the mail, holding it in your hands, opening it, sitting down and reading it makes it a one-on-one experience.

   With the direct mail, you can't be distracted by the internet, Twitter or Facebook. You can't click to go to another website. You can't lose the file on your computer. It physically sits around your house and you are reminded of it over and over. You will look at it and read it and direct mail beats the piss out of email in response rates.

   With enormous email deliverability rates these days, if you send an email to 1,000 people, only about 10% really open and read it. Fifty percent often don't even GET YOUR EMAIL because of the spam filters. That is a high bounce rate. Sometimes the read rate is as low as 5% or

1%. You may think a lot of people are reading your newsletter by email, but very few are. Direct mail works a lot better.

Even MORE Good Reasons to Send a Monthly Physical Newsletter

Did you know a paper newsletter is just like a newsPAPER or MAGAZINE that you control? You can put a special offer in your newsletter, each month or every few months. How about offsetting the cost or even profiting from sending it out by advertising the legal practice of someone in a different practice area? (ex: You do DUI. They do divorce.)

Consider: Why not sell cheap advertising space to a dentist, chiropractor, tax prep person or estate planner? These people can totally offset the cost of your mailing by paying you to advertise in your mailer.

Tell a dentist you mail to 400 people once a month. Charge him $99 a month to put an ad in for dentistry. How's THAT for cheap, effective advertising?

Newsletters are cheap, effective and an excellent way of mining your old client list; clients you mistakenly thought were dead, gone and unable to help you! They can make you a LOT more money than you ever imagined.

WHEN OR HOW TO ADVERTISE ON GOOGLE ADWORDS WITHOUT LOSING YOUR SHIRT

Everyone has either heard of or tried Google pay-per-click (PPC) (Aka Google Adwords). No, not paperclips that you use to hold paper together, but pay-per-click, like you do with a mouse. Click, click, and click.

Watch out, because Google pay-per-click service can empty your wallet faster than any strip club ever could, leaving you "frustrated" all the same.

Most attorneys that try it, get burned pretty quickly. Surely it's alluring because PPC promises immediate clicks, calls, clients, and floods of traffic. That is how it's sold. However, it is a very dangerous, expensive, and competitive arena to play in. I'm here to tell you what to do so you don't get burned, and limp away thinking, "Google Adwords doesn't work".

First of all, you're probably going to shy away from its complexity and hire a 'Google-Certified PPC Firm'. Bad, bad move 90% of the time. Why?

Nearly all the PPC firms that I've worked with use THEIR account to run your AdWords campaigns, not YOUR OWN

ACCOUNT. This means you're going to get filtered, useless information through a 3rd party that's unverifiable.

You say you don't care. You just want the phone to ring?

Good luck there, buddy. Without a way to track your PPC spending and match it with phone calls or contact form submissions on your website, you're begging to be taken for a ride twice – once by the PPC provider, and again by Google itself.

Do you know that your "budget" (let's say $1,500 a month) gets allocated partly to pay the PPC Company and partly to advertise for clicks? How much dough actually goes towards paying for clicks? You'll never know. It could be 80%, could easily be 30% - it's often 50% or less.

No reason on earth why you can't have your own PPC account, provide the login and password to a PPC provider and have them run it for you…

"Sir, that's not how we do things at XYZ Adwords Company. Don't worry, our proprietary, baloney dashboard will show you this and that, and blow smoke up your behind… I mean, uh, show you floods of traffic and all the calls you're getting from advertising."

If you hear this kind of garbage, don't hire the company. Anyone that doesn't allow YOU to use YOUR OWN account, so you can log in anytime and verify first hand what's going on, is playing you for a sucker.

Typical rates for REAL PPC companies that actually know what they're doing are 20% of spend, and in addition, you pay them separately from your spend / budget.

How Complicated IS Google Adwords?

Google pay-per-click <u>looks really simple</u> but is extremely complicated; like trying to fly a 747 Jet Plane.

Hundreds of controls, levers, dials, specifications are possible:

- You can choose to advertise in a specific geographic area, (ex: an 8-mile radius around your office)
- You can choose different keywords. Let's say you're in Atlanta, Georgia, for example. You can choose keywords such as "Atlanta Personal Injury Lawyer,"; "Discount Atlanta Personal Injury Attorney"; "Atlanta DUI Lawyer" or "Best Atlanta Sex Crimes Attorney."
- Should you bid on a few keywords or hundreds? Which ones?
- How much will you pay to bid on a keyword? Will you pay more on some vs. others?
- What times of day will you advertise? 24/7? Just office hours? Only Sunday through Tuesday, 7am-7pm?
- Do you know what negative keywords you're going to start out with? (Keywords that trigger your ads NOT to show up. Ex: "free" "cheap" "pro bono")
- Will your ads show on laptops, smartphones, ipads, or just desktops?

- How many different ads are you going to test? Which ad goes with which keyword? How will you know if one ad is "better" than the other?
- Do you know how to track and tie a click on your ad to an actual phone call or a submitted contact form?
- Where will your ad appear on the page? Bottom or top? How much will you have to pay per click to get a certain position on the page?
- <u>Troubleshooting:</u> Google PPC is a fickle beast – malfunctions ALL THE TIME. Things don't work as planned – can you diagnose what's going on and fix it?
- How much is your daily and monthly budget? How many clicks will it take to get someone to call or email on average?
- How much do you have to spend to retain a client, on average? Is that number $400? Is it $3,000? Is that 'expensive' or 'worth it'? Does it bring you ROI?
- How much does it cost to get a click? Is your market $10 a click or is it $20 a click? Can you even begin to afford that?

Is this complex enough for you? Do you have the time to even scratch the surface and put together a campaign that will make sense, not rob you blind and actually **make you money**?

Welcome to the Google Adwords Strip Club, where daily ad spend budgets, to even be let in the door, typically run $50 - $100 a day; which translates to $1,500 - $3,000 a month.

A lot of markets, such as DUI or criminal defense are horrifically expensive, running $8, $15, $30, even $40 a click.

A daily budget of $100 can easily be eaten up with a meager useless 10 clicks or less. I've seen it happen many times.

Some major metros have such competitive, rabid markets, that you could blow $100 by 10am and miss out on all the relevant potentials traffic later in the day. Your monthly budget could easily run out the first week, and then you have no more money for the month. This is a serious game for serious players and requires extensive knowledge to run properly.

How to Run Google Adwords the Right Way & Figure Out if It's Profitable or Not

Instead of terrifying you with all the complications of Google Adwords, I'll give you some insight into how to run a successful campaign with the actual hope of making money... OR, figure out quickly that this form of advertising is NOT working for you and quit before you go broke.

In Google PPC, the ads you write are one of the biggest drivers of success vs. failure. The typical, 'me-too' ads that say that same junk as everyone else: "We'll fight for you," "Call today," "24-hour free consultation" will get lost in the noise and do nothing for you.

In other advertising mediums, this may give you mediocre results, but in Google Adwords, this will get you absolutely nowhere.

Google is a harsh mistress. It punishes crappy advertisers with higher pay per click prices, low traffic, and no profit if you don't have compelling ads that get clicked on more than your competitions' ads.

Think Google cares about your money? Not a bit. Google makes in the neighborhood of $40 BILLION a year, and you're a cockroach to be stepped on, not catered to.

Google's mission is to provide the most relevant search results to people Googling stuff. It's the most competitive ad space on planet Earth. Punishing you with higher costs that drive you out is a part of the game – there are tons of other advertisers that you're competing against in this space.

Their theory is that a good ad serves their customers better and attracts more clicks. Coincidentally, clicks always cost more in the beginning because you are building an account history that Googles' computers and technicians are evaluating.

The ad itself is very critical. The right ad can make you money and the wrong ad can lose you money. You have to come up with ethical, creative ads that address, within a microsecond, what potentials are looking for. It's not an easy thing to do.

Typical *'click-through rates' are a measly 1%* (ratio of # of times your ad appears in search vs. the # of people that clicked). Once someone clicks on your ad, they come to a "landing page" – a certain page on your website. (99% of attorneys send clickers to their homepage).

Let's say your law practice does criminal defense, DUI and car accidents. Also, you have three different attorneys at your firm, each of whom handles a different area of law.

Sending a potential that clicked on a DUI ad to a homepage with three different practice areas is more distracting than helpful.

You want to send the potential to a custom page that immediately addresses what they clicked on. If they clicked on a DUI ad, send them to a DUI-specific page.

If they click on a car accident ad, send them to a page on car accidents. You can get even more specific than that. Let's say you're targeting the 1st time DUI offenders. Instead of sending clickers to a generic DUI page, it's best to send them to a "What you must know about 1st time DUI" page, right?

The more specific you can make your whole sales process using Google Adwords, the better your results.

Remember, customers go through a progression of "googling something". They are eyeballing ads, clicking on a compelling one, landing on a relevant or non-relevant page, then either engaging, reading and calling you, or clicking the back button and wasting your money and their time… on to a million other competitor websites they go!

How to Choose a Worthwhile Google PPC Management Company and Not Get Burned

Most Google PPC companies function to take your money and keep you in the dark. Never, ever, ever, ever use anything but your own Google Adwords account to which you provide access to the PPC Company.

Here's what to ask:

First say, "I am going to give you access to my pay-per-click account. I don't want your pay-per-click account. You use mine."

If they won't do this, walk away. You want to own the account and provide access to the company. Make sure you can lock them out if they don't do their job. If they can work with your PPC account, then you may ask the subsequent questions.

- Do you split test ads? Do you write different ad copy? How often will you change my ads up?
- What keywords are you proposing to bid on?
- What negative keywords are you going to use?
- What geography, times of day, and days of the week do you propose for best results?
- How much are your fees? (standard is 20% of spend)
- What do you suggest for my budget and why?
- What's the average cost per click for my chosen markets?
- Do you provide month to month service or require a long-term contract? (it WILL take 30-60 days to test and ramp up a campaign, but never sign more than a 6-month agreement – no reason to do it at all)
- Do you create and split test landing pages? Do you know what a landing page is?
- Do you know what broad, phrase or exact match is?
- Do you set up conversion tracking? (A conversion is a phone call or a contact form filled out) (Can you tie back a

specific keyword to the ad that was clicked to the phone call that was generated?)

- Are you Google Certified? (Meaningless, but ask anyway!)
- Have you worked on attorney PPC campaigns before, specifically in my practice areas?
- Will you tell me if pay-per-click is just not working for me? (Yeah, good luck getting someone you pay to tell you it is not working for you – might as well ask them to freak out)

Honestly, I would actually look for a full-fledged, marketing consulting company; not just a pay-per-click only company.

You want someone that does SEO, pay-per-click, direct mail, newsletters; the whole boat – someone that specializes in attorney marketing.

You may ask me: "**Why?**"

A multi-faceted, attorney specialist marketing company is **incentivized to say**, "All right, we tried pay-per-click. It didn't work. Let's move on to something else that will work."

They're not married to pay-per-click, nor are they a one-trick pony where if pay-per-click doesn't work, they have nothing else to offer except being fired. A pay per click only company will never, ever tell you that Adwords isn't working – it's against their interest to do so.

Yes, Google Adwords CAN WORK for law attorneys. It's not impossible. It's actually quite do-able and potentially profitable... IF you get experienced help and know at least the basics of how it works.

Google Adwords essentially requires a "$2,000 - $4,000 tuition" to be paid before you can expect profitable results. Sad, but true.

Don't think that you'll ever get anywhere with Google Adwords if you don't track phone and web contact form conversions. You might as well throw your money out the window at 60 mph.

Watch out, because Google Adwords can be far worse than visiting Disneyworld and spending 4x what you intend to spend (this is a documented fact, that most Disneyworld visitors spend 4x what they intend), yet STILL coming away with nothing.

Maintaining Profitable Retainer Fees Without Cutting Your Own Throat

Pricing your services is a huge issue; especially in the bad economy of the past six years.

I've done studies and I can tell you that prices vary drastically not only by the metro area but by the attorney themselves!

In your city, at this very moment, there are DUI attorneys charging $750, while right down the street, others are charging $3,000.

All of these guys co-exist in the same city. They see the same potential audience of clients.

While some lawyers are starving to death, some gross $500,000 a year. There's a LOT that needs to be said about price and pricing your services without cutting your own throat.

First of all: **Never be the lowest cost attorney. Ever.**

I think you already know that deep, down inside. Yes, there's a lot of pressure from competition squawking low prices and $500 down to start your case. The economy sucks. Potential clients beat you up on price and the entire world seems to be on a payment plan.

Trust me, bad advertising is everywhere. There are plenty of attorneys in your market that will sooner kill it versus make any real money. They are offering DUI's starting at $750. Bankruptcies are going for $400 down, or all misdemeanors starting at $1,500. Ignore their futile advertising because they will go into a death spiral and drag you down with them if you let yourself be swayed.

No one can do a good job, working for a pauper's wage. Deep down even the potentials know this.

When you talk to potential clients, you have to be prepared to defend your price. You know, better than I do, that this "elephant in the room" is permanently parked there; just waiting to be recognized, at each and every consultation.

Let's say you charge $3,000 for a 1ˢᵗ time DUI case with no trial anticipated, and competition is quoting $1,500.

Potential clients naturally think, "Attorney XYZ only charges $1,500, and this guy (you) is quoting me $3,000. Is it really worth it to spend that extra money?"

Even if they don't voice this concern, <u>it IS on their mind</u>. You have to address it, defend it, prepare your case for the 'price jury' and be ready, just like a court case. If you don't have a prepared script or set of statements you can use anytime you talk to a potential client to justify your price, you're asking for trouble.

Easy to say, but hard to do. You may ask me: "How DO I defend price or make it a non-issue before its dark specter is raised?"

One way I've seen "A"-level marketers do this, (which I think is fantastic), is to first build up the value of their services to 3, 5, or 10x what they are asking a client to pay. They show clients that number and then discount way down and then show them the final numbers.

I will go into this strategy in a lot more depth shortly, (also, see attached sample worksheet) but for now, that is the basic structure.

Remember, you're not just justifying your price, you're also battling "private attorney vs. public defender vs. no attorney".

Do you have a prepared and compelling argument as to why it is a horrible idea for potential clients to defend themselves?

Why should someone hire you versus use a public defender or look for legal aid services?

How about hiring your competition versus you? What makes YOU so unique and special that you CAN command a certain price?

Typical arguments aren't going to cut it, especially in today's highly competitive, zero attention span, marketed-to-by everybody world, in which potential clients live.

"You get what you pay for."

"I'm not the cheapest in town."
"I'm aggressive."
"I care about my clients."

Not very compelling. I'm sorry, but that's boilerplate.

How about the following statements:
"I deliberately limit the number of clients I take. This allows me to spend a lot of personal time on your case. I can delve way deep into the issues and find every possible defense to your case, to the point of overkill."

"I'll attend every court date – no junior associates here will suddenly appear in court with your file in hand and with no personal knowledge of your case."

"I'll never just throw you under the bus to get you sign a plea agreement. Only after we've exhausted every possible alternative will we plea your case out."

"I charge what I feel is a reasonable rate, especially since the alternative of losing costs five times more than I charge."

"I've overseen 700+ cases. The judges, prosecutors, and court personnel know me, and I know how the local court's function and their peculiarities. I know which judges tend to rule this way versus that way and which prosecutors tend to agree to this versus that. We have a mutual respect for each other, and that benefits you tremendously in court."

If you make a compelling offer to a potential client, you just may avoid the money excuses that they give, and cut off potential reservations before they voice them or leave your office, never to return.

Many potential clients won't even tell you that they think you're too expensive. However, they will think it if you don't make preparations, and they won't hire you because of a lack of preparation.

Potential clients may say, "You're too expensive," or "That's a lot of money," or maybe "I don't have any money."

Statements like these are defense mechanisms, and often do not mean they don't have money. Take notice of when you hear protestations about price. In what situation are you hearing them? What was your conversation like?

It's often because you haven't prepared them sufficiently and allayed their fears that they're making not only the best choice but the obvious and ONLY choice that will get them the result, which they desperately need.

The way you talk to clients in person, through email, text message, and on the phone is very important and either sways them towards or away from you. Show them so much value that _**you are their clear choice to hire**_, versus everyone else in your market.

The better you are at preparing for and defusing pricing objections, the more potentials you'll retain, the more selective you'll become, and best of all? You can charge a heck of a lot more, have fewer clients, make the same or greater money, and be the envy of your fellow attorney brethren.

Read on for a specific example how to present your value and subsequent price, based on marketing gurus' best practices.

A GREAT WAY TO COMBAT, "I HAVE NO MONEY", "YOU'RE TOO EXPENSIVE", OR "I CAN'T AFFORD IT"

Why the statements like, "I don't have any money,"; "I don't have enough money," or "You're too expensive," no longer have to derail your retention process.

You spend time, effort and serious money just to get potential clients to agree to and show up for an initial in-office consultation. On average, smart lawyers like you spend $600-$1,000 in marketing, staff time, and your time, just to get someone in the door.

Sadly, at the end of an initial consultation (that cost you so dearly just to get) you run into pricing issues, and many times, have no good defense on why your prices are high enough to earn a good return.

I surveyed 38 attorneys on what they do to combat pricing objections like these. Pricing pressure is pretty pervasive (PPPP) and sadly can put your law practice into a death spiral quickly.

Of course, you don't want to take on clients that truly have no money. So, initial upfront screening can help dramatically.

However, when potential clients say, "I don't enough money,"; "You're too expensive," or "I don't have any money," many times it is because you haven't built enough trust or value to differentiate yourself as the OBVIOUS CHOICE when potentials are shopping attorneys for their case.

The trick is to build trust, rapport, likeability, and authority in a prospect's mind BEFORE you reveal your price. If you've sufficiently built up enough value, when you reveal your price, hiring YOU will be cheap in comparison to any and every other alternative.

Top marketing gurus go through this exact flow when pitching people to buy their products, so you can learn a lot from studying them as I have.

By attending a lot of marketing seminars, getting pitched by the best in the world, and coughing up $1,000-$3,000, I discovered their secrets. Many of these secrets I share here that you can use in your own law practice to retain more clients, while charging premium prices. The way they pitch is always the same, but it works.

See the document on the next page which talks about the total cost of a DUI conviction. Let's go through it and I'll show you how to build value in the eyes of clients.

Attorney Marketing Association

Report of findings: Total cost of a DUI / DWI Conviction
(1st offense; national average; non aggravated; low BAC .08-.15)

Initial Vehicle Tow & Impound	$250
Bail Bond fees (if applicable; 10% of bond amt)	$250
Transport from Jail	$50
Request to Dispute Administrative Hearing (re: Driver License Suspension)	$110
Court Fees, Fines, Penalties	$1,250
Court Fee for Pleading Guilty	$250
Driver's License Suspension (avg 180 days) & Alternate Transportation Cost (taxi, bus) (avg $17 / day * 5 days/wk * 24 weeks)	$3,060
Increased Auto Insurance Premiums (avg 3 yrs of $116 / month increase)	$4,176
Driver's License Reinstatement Fees After Suspension is Completed	$375
Probation Costs ($250/mo * 12 months avg)	$3,000
Decreased Earning Ability Due to Criminal Conviction w/ avg 10 year Expungement if available ($10,000 a year * 10 years)	$100,000 ???
Expungement of Criminal Record (if available)	$1,500 ???

Total National Average Cost Estimate (Source: AMA)   **$12,771**
(1st offense; non-aggravated; low blood alcohol level .08 - .15)

Bankrate.com's Total Cost of a DUI Calculation: $9,000 - $24,000
http://www.bankrate.com/finance/personal-finance/dui-memorial-day-20-000-1.aspx

MSNBC Money Magazine's Total Cost of a DUI Calculation: $10,000
http://money.msn.com/auto-insurance/dui-the-10000-dollar-ride-home.aspx

With a potential client, take this sheet out at the end of your consult or even in the beginning, depending on how you want to structure your pitch.

The end results will be determined by demonstrating that your fee is much lower **than the price they would _have to pay_** if convicted. No, you can't guarantee an outcome, but a sore loser bet is far worse than a decent likelihood of mitigating their charges and circumstances.

When you walk a potential client through the sheet above, they'll perceive your services in a totally different way. They'll no longer think you're "expensive". They won't think, "I don't have money".

They'll realize, "I have GOT TO get money to hire this attorney to defend me because it's OBVIOUS that what he offers has 2, 3, or 5x the value of being convicted. In fact, I'm saving money by hiring him, not spending."

(Your local grocery store uses "Saving vs. Spending" language, and now you know why)

I recommend introducing this document both at the beginning of some consultations and at the end of others, to test which is more effective for your practise. Your admin can go through the document if you're uncomfortable or unwilling to do it. Some attorneys do have their admins talk prices so that clients won't perceive them as the bad guy – instead, the secretary is the bad guy.

Now here's what you need to do: Pull out this document and say, "I want to show you a comparison of costs for pleading guilty or defending yourself versus hiring a private attorney with years of experience like me. You'll be shocked at the price difference."

Now go through each of the line items, one by one in detail to arrive at the bottom price. As you step through the items, ask: "Does this make sense to you?"

Get them to agree to the potential cost of each item, and they'll readily agree to the bottom line number.

At the bottom, point to the number the red arrow points to – even circle it with a red pen for effect. Now have them look at the references below it.

Then say, "Here are three references from three neutral third parties showing the total cost of a DUI conviction (adapt this document for any particular crime!) A reasonable person would certainly agree that I could charge that amount but personally, I think that would be ridiculous. My job is to get you results without draining your bank account."

Now put a big, red slash through that number and say, "I'm not going to charge you that amount. Heck, I'm not even going to charge you half that amount."

"For the work and time I'm going to put in defending your case, and to help you avoid paying this huge amount of money, I'm only going to charge you (a third or a quarter of that amount)." As you say this, write down your price.

"I may not be able to get your case thrown out or your charges reduced. However, it's likely I can make a pretty serious dent, and help you avoid paying this huge number that you'd likely pay if you pled guilty, represented yourself, or had a public defender who doesn't have much time to spend on your case.

I'm stepping you through this document so you're fully informed **what you're getting &why I charge what I do.** I think you see the tremendous value, bargain, and discount my fee asks, and people agree it's worth it in spades."

So that's the spiel. How do you think the potential client will perceive this? It works like magic and you have to try this script. What you're doing without saying anything is starting with a much higher number that comes NOT FROM YOU, but from a third party, authoritative sources. The potential client becomes anchored to the $12,000 price that you're building up for them, step by step. You then step in to save the day, cross it out and put your minuscule retainer fee in comparison.

NOW, when you need to take the discussion a step further if a payment plan is needed, for instance…

Write down your retainer fee; (ex: $2,500). "I'm not going to stop there. Because you're telling me money is tight, we can do just two payments of $1,250 (or 3 payments of $833)."

"You're getting $12,000 of value for an unbeatable price."

Building up the value, then coming back down to your retainer is going to cause a **very different reaction** in your prospect's mind versus if you went through the whole consult, then just asked for your retainer at the end with no VALUE BUILD up first.

Don't be afraid to try this both at the beginning and at the end of your consultations, and let me know how much it boosts your retention rates and lowers price resistance from potentials.

To build up your value, you may want to have your admin go through this first **before the potential even sees you for the consult**. Your admin can also do this at the end.

Utilize price strategy from the pros, like I did!

WHAT TO DO NEXT

I often hear the follow, puzzling comment from attorneys who read this book:

"Rich, I read your entire Secrets of Attorney Marketing book cover to cover and I loved it. Now, how can you help me in my law practice?"

When I started hearing this, I was confused... if someone just read my entire book cover to cover, why were they asking me to help them in their law practice? After all, I wrote this book with full disclosure of how to grow your law practice. Did I not make it easy enough to understand what to do?

I realized that teaching marketing was not enough. Attorneys are busy, especially successful ones.

They want <u>Done-For-You</u> marketing that requires as little of their time and involvement as possible.

That's when I started offering a complimentary, 15 minute phone strategy session where interested lawyers can explain their current marketing, strategy and results, and get a specific, detailed plan of how Speakeasy Marketing can help them grow their law firm.

<u>**I invite you to request a complimentary strategy session**</u> (it's <u>not</u> a sales call in disguise) by emailing or calling:

richard.jacobs@speakeasymarketinginc.com

(888) 570-7338